THE TRAVELERS' GUIDE TO
AFRICAN CUSTOMS AND MANNERS

Also by the authors:

The Travelers' Guide to European Customs and Manners
The Travelers' Guide to Asian Customs and Manners
The Travelers' Guide to Latin American Customs and Manners
The Travelers' Guide to Middle Eastern Customs and Manners

THE TRAVELERS' GUIDE TO
AFRICAN CUSTOMS
AND MANNERS

Elizabeth Devine
and
Nancy L. Braganti

St. Martin's Press
New York

Illustrations by Raquel Jaramillo

Maps by Fred Haynes

Library of Congress Cataloging-in-Publication Data

Devine, Elizabeth, 1938–
    The travelers' guide to African customs & manners / Elizabeth Devine and Nancy L. Braganti.
        p.   cm.
    ISBN 0-312-11909-7
    1. Africa, Sub-Saharan—Guidebooks.   2. Africa, Sub-Saharan—Social life and customs.   I. Braganti, Nancy L., 1941– .   II. Title.
DT349.8.D48   1995
390'.0967—dc20   94-43550
                                                                                      CIP

First edition: March 1995

10   9   8   7   6   5   4   3   2   1

In memory of Mary Ellen Falck,
a true friend . . .
Ti volevo tanto bene

N.L.B.

To Daniel,
with thanks for some of life's best laughs,
and
to George,
raconteur extraordinaire

E.D.

CONTENTS

ACKNOWLEDGMENTS

We wish to thank the following for helping us to prepare this book: Hassat Abiola, Matti Amadhila, Margherite Dean Armstrong, Femi Awotesu, Joanne Bennett, Nancy Benson, Karen Blythe, Barbara Brown, Rosemary Chimdganda, Elizabeth Colliard, Robert Cooper, Ruth Cooper, Sheila Crane, Caroline Doughty, Keith Doughty, Rosemary Esin, Ruth Fig, Ann Flack, Karanja Gakio, Elizabeth Gannon, Janet Ghattas, Anna Goertz, Penny Hamilton, Brooke Hammond, Jonathan Haynes, Luisa Heffernan, Rick Heffernan, Julie Huffaker, Julie Jalelian, Faith Kasirye, Joyce Kegelis, Siga Diocoran Keita, Amy Kessel, Susan Liebold, Kevin Lowther, Sara MacCarthy, Mary Marro, Martha Mhalanga, Hope Mugerwa, Muburu Musoke, Cara Nelson, Robert Newman, Peter Ngaiza, Relendis Oben, John Ofori, Frances Onipede, Alexander Pancic, Joseph D. Policano, Mark Rosenthal, Anne Salmond, Elizabeth Sarkodie-Mensah, Mamadou Lamine Savadogo, South African Tourism Board, Dorothy Stephens, Carl Stinson, Nathaniel Stone, Christine Summers, Seth Tyler, Roger Vinita, Karen L. Weber, Edward Wheatley, World Learning (founded as the U.S. Experiment in International Living), Cheryl Zoll. We also would like to thank those who assisted but prefer to remain anonymous.

And last—but never least—we would like to thank our wise and supportive editor, Barbara Anderson.

THE TRAVELERS' GUIDE TO
AFRICAN CUSTOMS AND MANNERS

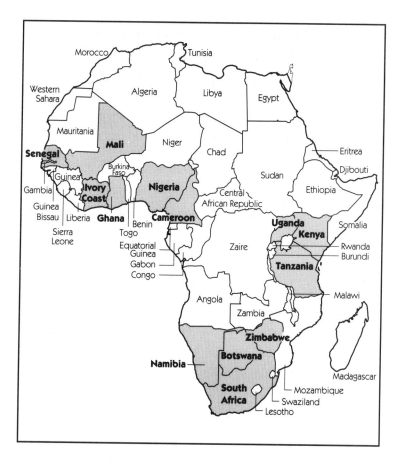

INTRODUCTION

Perhaps it was Marlin Perkins. Sitting in front of the black-and-white TV in the 1950s, watching Perkins on *Zoo Parade* show us elephants and tigers, animals we thought we would never see outside a zoo, we became fascinated with Africa.

Now, it seems almost weekly, brochures arrive from zoos or museums offering the opportunity to visit Botswana or Kenya to view the wildlife. One young friend, who visited the Serengeti in Tanzania and was awe-struck by its wildlife and its beauty, is searching for a career that will allow him to return there.

Though the guidebook publishers are beginning to catch up with the interest in Africa, they don't tell you how the people of the many cultures represented on the continent will behave toward you and how you should behave toward them. *The Travelers' Guide to African Customs and Manners* will fill that gap for you.

For easy reference, the book is divided by country, and in each country we cover a series of topics:

Greetings: While the custom of handshaking prevails, the handshake itself is different from the one to which Westerners are accustomed. We'll describe the handshake of each country. In all countries, people don't shake hands as firmly as North Americans do. Be sure you don't crush the hand of the person you're greeting.

In social settings men should shake hands with all the men in the group when arriving and when departing. If a woman offers her hand, shake it. Don't offer yours first.

What's most important to remember about greetings is that in most countries they go on for a *very* long time, and you will be regarded as *very* rude if you try to shorten your greeting.

Conversation: We'll tell you what the country's official language is, as well as the one that's most widely spoken—often they are not the same. Swahili is spoken throughout East Africa, from Kenya and Tanzania through Zaire. If you're going to East Africa, bring along Robert Leonard's excellent *Swahili Phrasebook* (Berkeley, CA: Lonely Planet Publications, 1988).

In northern Mali, northern Nigeria, and northern Cameroon, many, many people speak Fulani or Fulfoulde, the common market language. Each country has an individual language, but all speak this common market language, thus facilitating business and trade.

From colonial days, French and English linger as second languages, sometimes as a country's official language. The French-speaking countries included in this book are Cameroon, Côte d'Ivoire (Ivory Coast), Mali, and Senegal.

Everyone at some time has fallen into one of life's conversational potholes. We will try to help you sidestep them by warning you about subjects to avoid (e.g., questions regarded as too personal or questions that could cause political trouble for an African).

A little problem you may encounter: Since agreeing with others is a sign of respect, people frequently reply "yes" to a request, even though they won't be able to fulfill it. For example, they may accept an invitation, while knowing they won't be able to attend the event. One way of dealing with this difficulty is to avoid "yes" or "no" questions.

A solution to the above difficulty would be to inquire what the people are doing that day to learn if it's feasible for them to come. Then offer the invitation. If they don't appear as invited, try not to be angry. Their respect for you didn't allow them to say "no" to the invitation.

Telephones: Here you'll find advice about making calls from public phones. Unfortunately, it's not easy. In most African countries, the public phones you'll find on the streets are broken.

Your best bet is to go to the post office and call from there. (It also frees you from having to keep dropping change in the phone to prolong a call.) Bring plenty of reading material, because the wait for a call to go through can be long.

Calling from North America or Europe to Africa is easier and less expensive than the reverse. The easiest time to get a line from Africa to call abroad is between 5:00 P.M. and 6:00 A.M., African time.

In Public: In this section, we offer advice on how to treat other people so as not to offend them, and on how to gain their approval.

Where British and French colonial interests were strong, conservative attitudes prevail in terms of behavior and dress, especially in Southern Africa.

Because of the spread of Islam to West Africa, traditional values are preserved there—i.e., men can't act in any way to disgrace their families; people are more discreet; there is less drunkenness and AIDS, and there are fewer violent crimes. However, some Muslims in Africa are not so rigid as those in the Middle East.

Some travelers try to get a touch of home by having mail sent *poste restante* or to American Express. If you are one of them, make sure that the person writing to you prints your last name in all capital letters and then underlines it. If you are expecting a letter, and the clerks can't find it, ask them to check under your first name also.

If you want to make a hit, especially with children, bring an instant camera. Take one picture to give to them, and take another to keep yourself. If you're traveling with another person, consider using two cameras: one of you can take instant pictures and give them to the people, and the other can get more interesting candid shots with the second camera. (Of course a single person can do this, if he/she doesn't mind a bit of a juggling act.)

Don't be surprised if people want money in return for being photographed. This is almost invariably true with the Masai.

Many of us from the West find it difficult to get used to bargaining, the customary method of arriving at a price in much of the world. We may get a bit embarrassed haggling over prices, especially when the first price is relatively low. In most of Africa, however, it's considered gauche *not* to bargain, because the encounter is regarded as a social event. (In the individual chapters, we've pointed out places where bargaining is not practiced.)

Two issues you will surely have to deal with in public are poverty and begging. To ease your feelings about poverty, buy crafts from street vendors, pay shoeshine boys to polish your shoes, and give money to street entertainers.

Begging is an integral part of many African cultures. You'll have to decide whether to give to most, to none, or to some. You may wish to give to the elderly and to handicapped adults. If you want to give to children, it's best to offer a small gift—e.g., pens, pencils, balloons, stickers, colored Band-Aids.

A Note on Safaris: You must first choose the type of safari you want—an active experience, such as walking or camping out—or one in which you're in a vehicle (possibly an airplane for one of the flying safaris). Many types of accommodations are available for safaris, from luxurious lodges to simple tents.

Tanzania has the largest wildlife migration in the world. The best time to view it is from December to May in the Serengeti. However, you may want to avoid December and January, as well as July and August, in both Tanzania and Kenya, because the tourist season is at its peak.

You'll be allowed only one bag on safari. Bring insect repellent, sun block, binoculars, sunglasses, a flashlight, any prescription medicines you take, twice as much film (high-speed) as you think you'll need, a zoom lens, a bathing suit for swimming pools, and long-sleeved shirts and long pants to guard against the sun and protect against insects. Bring outfits in neutral colors, since bright colors scare animals away. Many game lodges are at high altitudes, and evenings can be cold, so be sure to include a sweater and/or jacket among your clothes. Bring *very* sturdy shoes.

Most often, you'll watch the game run from a van. No walking around is allowed until you reach your hotel or lodge. Heed the warning not to leave the van. Some animals—such as hippos—can be dangerous.

Roads can be very bumpy, since most are unpaved. If you have back problems or arthritis, you could have serious difficulties.

In Kenya and Tanzania, the Flying Doctors Association evacuates emergency cases by plane from remote areas. If you wish to have access to this service in case of emergency, enroll by paying a small fee to your safari outfitter when you arrive.

Dress: The best advice is, "When in doubt, be conservative." In those countries with a large Muslim population, women should make a special effort to be conservative in costume.

We have pointed out in which countries people are pleased if you wear their traditional costumes and in which countries they find it offensive.

In general, don't wear a safari suit, comfortable though it might be, for business, because that costume at a business meeting would, as one African told us, "smack of colonialism."

You'll probably find that business dress is more formal in the English-speaking countries—men wear jackets and ties. The French-speaking countries tend to be less formal, especially during hot weather.

Meals: We start by telling at what times meals are usually served and what people normally eat.

If you've suffered the result of spicy food on other continents, you shouldn't have that complaint in Africa, where the cooking doesn't run to spicy dishes.

Be cautious, however, when drinking African beers, because they have a higher alcohol content than most American beers.

If you are in a French-speaking country and don't want to drink liquor, say, *J'ai mal au foie* (zhay mahl o fwa), meaning, "I have a liver problem."

Remember to use only your right hand for eating. If you're left-handed and the group is eating from a communal bowl, sit on your left hand so you won't be tempted to use it. The left hand is used for cleaning after performing toilet functions.

When thinking about dining out, keep in mind that the Lebanese food in French-speaking West Africa is very good, as is the Indian food in English-speaking East Africa.

Hotels: We'll try to prepare you for some of the eccentricities associated with African hotels. For example, don't count on a reservation being honored. Perhaps a convention of local government officials has arrived; everything and everyone else then takes a back seat.

If water and/or electricity go off in a town or city, they will go off even in the best hotels. Be prepared. Bring a flashlight and batteries. Ask about water when you check in, since sometimes it's only on at a certain time for a short period.

Tipping: To paraphrase Sir Walter Scott, "Breathes there a traveler with soul so dead/Who never to her(him)self has said/ I DON'T KNOW HOW MUCH TO TIP."

This section should alleviate some tipping *angst*. We have given amounts in U.S. dollar equivalents, so that you won't have to worry about fluctuating currencies in African countries—concerned that what was a substantial tip last week is peanuts today.

In general, Africans don't think of tipping in specific amounts or percentages. The richer you look, the more you'll be expected to tip.

Keep in mind that in most of Africa, hotel room attendants appreciate receiving the toiletries you have left over at the end of your trip. By pleasing the hotel room attendants, you may lighten your homeward-bound luggage (which we hope will be stuffed with African crafts).

Private Homes: Because most Africans are so hospitable and hotel accommodations are so scarce, you may find yourself staying with—or at least visiting—an African family.

In this section, we'll give you tips on how to be a good visitor or house guest, and we'll try to show how customs differ in cities and villages.

We'll have some remarks on gift giving; in Africa it's a very structured and important social ritual. People give gifts to people whom they respect and who are above them in social status. The belief is that if you have been fortunate, you should be willing to share. Foreigners are viewed as rich; therefore many people, including children, will ask for money.

Business: This section begins with information on when businesses, banks, government offices, and stores are open. In countries where the weather is hot, offices and stores sometimes shut down for two hours or so around noon.

We continue with information about the country's currency and follow up with information on business practices, including how to find business contacts; when and how to schedule appointments; what copying, telex, and fax facilities are available; the language in which business is conducted; the pace at which business proceeds (almost invariably, *very* slowly); who will make final decisions; and, finally, some suggestions for business entertaining.

Although Western businesspeople are accustomed to doing business via telephone, that strategy won't work in Africa. Africans find it difficult to trust people on the telephone. They want to meet with you in person, unless they know you well. *Never* try to conclude a deal on the phone.

You'll probably find government officials and businesspeople more formal in the English-speaking countries—e.g., Uganda and Kenya.

A bit of advice useful in almost any business setting: Always make small talk and be friendly with the secretary of the person you're dealing with. If he/she is "on your side," you will have an easier time accomplishing your aims.

If your company regularly sends women to conduct business negotiations, you might want to think twice if the business to be done is in Africa. African men aren't used to dealing with women in positions of power and may well be ill at ease in doing so.

Holidays and Special Occasions: While we've listed for you the national holidays of each country, don't be surprised to find a holiday declared "at the drop of a hat." Possibly the President is going to the airport, so a holiday is announced. Keep informed by listening to the radio.

There are both religious holidays, celebrated according to the Christian and Muslim calendars, and secular holidays.

In addition to Ramadan and the feast celebrating the end of Ramadan (*Id al-Fitr*), the Muslim community celebrates Tabaski (*Id al-Kabir*)—see the section on Islam in the Introduction.

Transportation: Public transportation in Africa ranges from pickup trucks with benches to the super-luxurious Blue Train in South Africa. This section has information on taxis, buses, and trains. We also advise about driving, which is to be avoided if at all possible, especially since you may be the target of poorly paid police in search of a bribe. It is much better to hire a car and driver.

If you decide to drive, remember that maps for some places are not available, and many streets aren't marked or their names have changed.

In countries colonized by the British, driving is on the left. In French-speaking countries, cars on the right have the right of way.

A Peace Corps volunteer, who used to ride a motorbike, classified animals as to how they react to vehicles: chickens go in any direction; goats will keep running ahead of you; sheep will just look at you; dogs will lie down in front of you on the road; pigs (the worst) will run alongside a motorbike for half a kilometer, possibly taking your front tire with them in the process.

Legal Matters, Health, and Safety: Good manners pay off when a problem arises with an African official. Never raise your voice, even when the situation becomes exasperating. Speaking softly is a sign of respect; the more softly one speaks, the greater respect one shows. Make the official feel that he/she is important by using "Sir" or "Madam." Compliment the country, their kindness, etc. Whatever your sex, demonstrating a helpless attitude may help. If all else fails, consider offering a complimentary gift.

Be circumspect when offering a gift of this kind. When extending the gift, say, "May I help you?" or "Would you like a bottle of whiskey?" Many people barely make a living wage and rely on such gifts to live.

To avoid eating risky foods that someone has offered you, follow the advice of Scott Graham in his excellent book, *Handle with Care: A Guide to Responsible Travel in Developing Countries* (Chicago: The Noble Press, 1991). Among his valuable suggestions is simply to say that you have stomach problems—the least offensive way to deal with the issue.

Before leaving North America, call the Centers for Disease Control in Atlanta, Georgia at (404) 332-4559 to learn about required immunizations or any health problems you may expect to encounter. Or you can call the office of the U.S. Public Health Service Quarantine Station nearest you: Chicago, (312) 686-2150; Honolulu, (808) 541-2552; Los Angeles, (213) 215-2365; Miami, (305) 526-2910; New York, (718) 917-1685; San Francisco, (415) 876-2872; Seattle, (206) 442-4519.

Canadians should write or call for the brochure "Travel and Health," which gives information about health precautions to take when traveling outside Canada. Address: Health and Welfare Canada, 5th Floor, Brooke Claxton Building, Tunney's Pasture, Ottawa, Canada K1A 0K9.

British travelers should ask their travel agents about health conditions, since the agents are updated frequently by the Department of Health and Social Security. Travelers may telephone the Department at (071) 407-5522 to ask for "Public Inquiries" (to learn of any updated health forecasts) and to request a copy of their booklet, "Protect Your Health Abroad."

To avoid illness on your trip or as an unpleasant souvenir on your return home, read about appropriate precautions and about recognizing symptoms of potentially serious diseases in *Travellers' Health* by Richard Dawood (Oxford and New York: Oxford University Press, 1986).

To learn about any political conflicts that may have erupted in various African countries, U.S. citizens should call the Citizen's Emergency Center for the U.S. Department of State at (202) 647-5225. For the same information, Canadians should call (613) 992-3705, and residents of Great Britain (071) 213-3666.

About 45 minutes before your plane lands, ask for an *unopened* can of soda. It will be especially helpful in countries where you can't drink the water. The weather may be very hot, and you'll be happy to have a refreshing drink.

Bring with you several photocopies of all your important documents (e.g., airline tickets, passport, credit cards) in case they are stolen.

Don't flash money. Keep a few bills in a pocket, but keep most of your money in a secure place, such as a money belt.

Key Phrases: For countries where English isn't widely understood, we've provided useful phrases with phonetic pronunciations.

SOME GENERAL ADVICE

There's no better way to enhance a trip than by immersing yourself in the culture of the country before you go there. Read, read, read. Read history. Read biography. Read fiction. Read Isak Dinesen's splendid memoirs and short stories. Read Elspeth Huxley, especially *The Flame Trees of Thika.* Local librarians usually love patrons who come to them and ask for recommendations. Ask one to help you find books on the countries you'll be visiting.

Electronic technology offers another opportunity. If you have a computer and modem and subscribe to any of the "on-line" services, use one of the Bulletin Boards to find a pen pal in the country to which you'll be traveling. You'll get information about the country no travel agent could give, and you may make a friend you'll want to visit.

A big mistake many travelers make is judging a country in comparison to their own. That things are different doesn't make them better or worse. For example, in many African countries, driving is on the left (as in Britain). North Americans sometimes find this pattern confusing and say that driving is on the "wrong" side of the road. Don't use such an expression. Roads don't have right and wrong sides; they simply have different sides.

Ask questions—and listen to the answers. Few people in the world don't love to be interviewed—in a non-pushy way—and fewer still aren't closet tour guides or restaurant critics. An almost sure way to make friends is to ask advice about what to see and places to eat.

Hard as it may sometimes be, *never* lose your sense of humor. Travel tragedies have a way of turning into great dinner party anecdotes.

SOME SPECIAL HEALTH CAUTIONS

• Consider EVERY body of water (whether you're thinking of drinking from it or swimming in it) a potential source of bilharzia—a parasitic disease that causes fatigue, extreme exhaustion, and even death. It's spread by snails who live at the edges of lakes and slow-moving rivers. The parasite moves on to people and attacks such vital organs as the liver.

• In most African countries malaria can be a problem. Start taking antimalarial drugs a week or two before you'll be in the area and continue for about a month afterward. Consult your physician or the Centers for Disease Control about timing and dosages.

• In *Africa on a Shoestring* (Berkeley, CA: Lonely Planet Publications, 1992), written by Geoff Crowther (and others), the authors point out that venereal disease and AIDS "are prevalent in Africa to a degree unfamiliar to most Western travelers." AIDS, they continue, "known colloquially in East Africa as 'Slim' . . . is prevalent in Burundi, Rwanda, Uganda, and Zaire but less so in Kenya and Tanzania." Richard Everist and Jon Murray add in their book *South Africa, Lesotho, and Swaziland: A Travel Survival Kit* (Berkeley, CA: Lonely Planet Publications, 1993) that "AIDS is certainly present and possibly widespread in the heterosexual community. Official attitudes aren't helping much. The Johannesburg police consider that carrying condoms is *prima facie* evidence that a woman is a prostitute."

Obviously celibacy is the only certain prevention of the sexual transmission of AIDS. If you do have sex, be sure to use a latex condom.

The two other ways to get AIDS are through tainted blood or dirty needles. As Crowther *et al.* point out, you have serious problems if you need a blood transfusion, since "blood donors in Africa are rarely, if ever, screened for AIDS."

If you need an injection, make **ABSOLUTELY** sure that the needle is new or properly sterilized. Crowther *et al.* advise buying your own needle. If you have a condition that you know will require an injection, bring a supply of needles with you, along with a letter from your doctor explaining that you require the needles.

SOME SPECIAL WORDS FOR WOMEN

If you're traveling alone, whether for business or pleasure, you might want to invest in an inexpensive wedding band. When people ask about your husband, say that he'll be joining you shortly. If you prefer a fib to a lie, respond to questions about your marital status by saying that you're engaged.

Wherever you are in Africa, you won't err by being conservative, whether in dress or behavior. Be especially sure that your dress is modest in traditional rural areas and in Muslim areas.

When traveling alone by bus or train, always try to sit next to a woman. She can serve as protection from harassment by local men. Offer to help carry her bundles, play with her baby, etc.

Everist and Murray (see above) advise that women traveling alone are a curiosity. They suggest that you seek counsel from local women as to what places are safe. "Unfortunately," they add, "many of them are likely to be appalled at the idea of lone travel and will do their best to discourage you with horrendous stories, often of dubious accuracy."

PACKING LIST

This list doesn't cover everything you'll want to bring, but let us suggest some important items. If your visit is limited to cities, you can count on finding toiletries and aspirin, but if you prefer a particular brand, bring it with you. If you're venturing into rural areas, take along everything you'll need. Wherever you are traveling, pack a hat to ward off the intense sun.

Medical Supplies: Be sure to bring a more-than-adequate supply of any prescription drugs (in their original containers, if possible) you may be taking. If you run out, you could be in trouble, since drugs are known by different names in different countries. Your best bet is to ask your physician to provide you with a detailed list—with generic names and dosage amounts—of all prescription drugs you are taking, plus duplicate prescriptions for those items. Always pack your medication in your carry-on bag for safety.

If you use birth control, bring an ample supply of what you use.

If you wear glasses, bring an extra pair as well as a copy of your prescription. Be sure to pack a pair of sunglasses.

Besides any medication you may be taking, bring an antidiarrheal medication and a broad-spectrum antibiotic to combat bacterial infection. You'll need a prescription for both.

Other items to consider bringing: aspirin or your favorite headache-fever remedy, an antacid, a laxative, a motion-sickness remedy, insect repellent, lotion for insect bites, sunscreen, a cream to relieve sunburn, an antibiotic ointment for cuts, Band-Aids, a decongestant, cough medicine, and a remedy for muscle pains. It's also wise to bring a thermometer. Women may wish to include remedies for menstrual cramps and vaginal yeast infections.

Toiletries: Shampoo, deodorant, toothbrush and toothpaste, soap powder or liquid for washing clothes, a portable clothesline that can be strung over a bathtub, a shower cap, a large supply of tissues (always carry some, since public washrooms often do not have toilet paper), and moist towelettes.

Supplies: A flashlight with batteries (and an extra supply of batteries), a hair dryer (one that works on both 110 and 220 volts), and a collapsible plastic cup.

Religions

ISLAM

Islam (which means "submission to the will of God") is at the center of the lives of Africa's Muslims. The traveler should be sensitive to and show respect for the often deeply held religious beliefs of Muslims.

A Muslim has five duties:

1. Prayer (usually private) five times daily. On Friday, the Muslim Sabbath, men gather at mosques at midday for prayer.

2. Giving alms to the poor.

3. Fasting during Ramadan.

4. Making a pilgrimage to Mecca.

5. A profession of faith—stating in front of two male Muslim witnesses that there is no God but Allah (which means "God") and that Mohammed is his prophet.

The call to prayer sounds five times each day from the minarets of mosques: *Fajr*—one hour before sunrise; *Dhuhr*—at noon; *Asr*—mid-afternoon; *Maghreb*—sunset; and *Isha*—about 90 minutes after sunset. If you have a Muslim driver or tour guide, be prepared for him to stop to pray.

One of the holiest periods in the Muslim calendar is Ramadan, which lasts for one month. Since Muslims use a lunar calendar, Ramadan falls eleven days earlier each year. During Ramadan, people abstain from food, drink, and tobacco from dawn until sunset. Muslims believe that fasting trains one in self-discipline and that it quiets the spirit, subdues the passions, and gives one a sense of unity with all Muslims. People often spend much of the day in mosques, praying and reading the Koran. A cannon is fired to announce the rising and setting of the sun. It is also fired two hours before sunset to give people time to prepare a meal. (The meal is eaten after sunset.)

If you are in a Muslim area during Ramadan, be sensitive to the feelings of people observing the holiday. No one will expect non-Muslims to observe the ban on drinking, smoking, and tobacco. They will, however, appreciate your sensitivity if you eat in private and refrain from eating, smoking, and drinking in the presence of Muslims.

On the twenty-ninth of Ramadan—when the new moon appears—Ramadan is over. The breaking of the fast begins, and for three days everyone stops working. On the first morning after Ramadan, families dress in their finest and go to mosque. They have a special midday meal at home (their first midday meal in a month). (The Feast of Breaking the Fast is called *Id al-Fitr.*)

Another important Muslim commemoration is *Id al-Kabir* (Feast of the Sacrifice—also called Tabaski), celebrated at the end of the pilgrimage to Mecca. It recognizes Abraham's willingness to sacrifice his son Ishmael. People kill a sheep, camel, or goat and share it with the poor.

Some other things to know about Islam:

• Devout Muslims may not shake hands with women.

• Eating pork and drinking alcohol are forbidden by Islamic law. Don't do either in the presence of a Muslim unless he does it first.

• If you wish to visit a mosque, remove your shoes. Some Mosques do not admit women, and others have a separate entrance for women.

• Don't step on a prayer mat on which someone is praying, and don't walk in front of or photograph someone who is praying. During a period of Muslim holy days, wear clothing in subdued colors.

• Never place the Koran on the floor or put anything on top of it.

• Keep in mind that, since giving alms to the poor is an important part of Islam, begging is an Islamic institution. Whether or not to give something to a beggar is an entirely personal decision.

TRADITIONAL RELIGIONS

Each of Africa's hundreds of ethnic groups adheres to its own religion, most of them animistic—accepting a Supreme Being and believing in reincarnation.

The best description of animism is that of Alex Newton in *Central Africa: A Travel Survival Kit* (Berkeley, CA: Lonely Planet Publications, 1994). Newton writes:

> *The Creator is considered to be too exalted to be concerned with humans. There are, however, numerous lesser deities with whom one can communicate, typically through sacrifices. . . .*
>
> *The lesser deities, who act as intermediaries between the Creator and mortals, are frequently terrifying, corresponding to natural phenomena or diseases. Africans pray to these deities in order to gain good health, bountiful harvest, and numerous children. . . .*

According to Newton, two other important elements in African animistic religions are ancestors and magic. Ancestors protect the tribe, and good magic, sought through the offices of medicine men or sorcerers, keeps the evil spirits at bay.

MISCELLANEOUS

• The best maps of Africa are those published by Michelin. Buy them before you leave, since they aren't available in Africa.

• For an excellent series of guides to the regions of Africa, pick up those published by Lonely Planet. They are thoroughly researched and well written.

We hope you'll share our fascination with Africa. Thanks, Marlin Perkins.

BOTSWANA

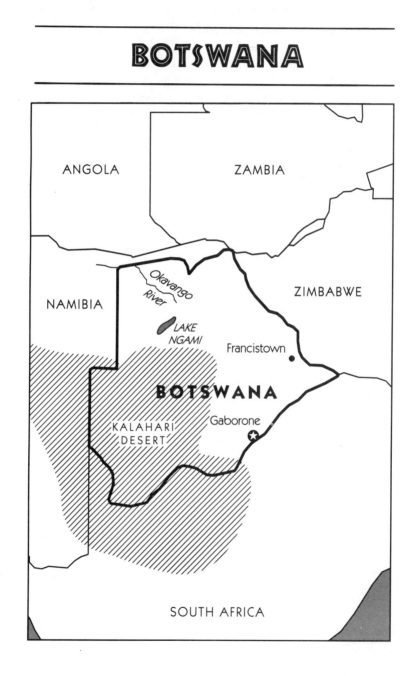

Just the name of the Kalahari desert conjures up images of adventure with abundant wildlife and desert sands. Indeed, the virtually uninhabited Kalahari occupies about 85% of the land in Botswana.

About 90% of the people of Botswana (one of the world's most sparsely populated nations) live along its eastern border. The growth in the urban population, since Botswana became an independent nation in the British Commonwealth in 1966, has been phenomenal.

Remember that while the country is Botswana, the people are called Batswana.

GREETINGS

• Note that there are two methods of handshaking: (1) With people you haven't met before or with superiors, shake with your right hand and hold *your* left hand under your right armpit. (2) Good friends of both sexes shake hands in a special way. Shake with your right hand and grab your own right arm above the wrist with your left hand. (Only Batswana who are highly Westernized will not use this handshake.)

• People usually shake hands when departing, as well as when greeting.

• When greeting a man of approximately your age, say "Doo-meh-lah-rah." When greeting a woman of your own age, say "Doo-meh-lah." These phrases mean: "Hello," "I agree," and "How are you?"

• When greeting an older man or a respected man, say "Doo-meh-lah rah-het-so." When greeting an older or a respected woman, say "Do-meh-lah mma-het-so." The phrases, which literally mean "old man" and "old woman," are used in a complimentary sense.

• Remember that if you are young, elders must introduce you if they choose to do so. A foreigner should always wait to be introduced. Don't hesitate to introduce yourself to a colleague, but never introduce yourself to the chief of a village, unless you are the only two in the room. In most situations, other people will introduce you.

• In business settings, use "Mr." or "Mrs.," even if a woman is not married. She will probably be flattered that you think she is married.

• To respect the Batswana's reserve, don't use first names until a Batswana does.

CONVERSATION

• English is the official language of Botswana, but the language understood by 90% of the people is Setswana, a Bantu language. Most professionals speak English, with varying degrees of skill.

• Avoid political discussions.

• A Batswana may ask you questions that you should not ask. Too many movies and a lack of contact have left a distorted view of America. Most Batswana think Americans are rich and violent and that the women are promiscuous. You may be asked how old you are, if you have a lover, and what your salary is. If you don't want to reveal this kind of information, you can invent a story. If you state your salary, you can then explain the cost of living in your country.

• Don't be surprised if Batswana claim that AIDS does not exist. They claim that it stands for American Invention to Discourage Sex.

• Good topics of conversation: (1) people's families—where they're from and from whom they're descended; (2) American and Botswana popular music; (3) drought (if there is one, and there usually is, it's a "hot" topic); (4) current events—most Batswana receive daily news in some form and discuss current world events; (5) South Africa—unless your views are racist.

• People love to tease and joke. For example, when a child falls down, other children may laugh. It's their way of reducing the fright associated with pain. However, if you deliberately laugh at someone or tease him, and he doesn't know that you're joking, he will be confused or insulted and refuse to speak to you. However, most Batswana go out of their way to excuse *faux pas* by foreigners.

• Note that Batswana appreciate compliments. It's the best way to assure someone that you are respectful and gracious—two qualities Batswana most appreciate.

• Should you insult someone (obviously unintentionally), he/

she may turn the head or the whole body away from you.

• Don't be surprised if people touch your chest while conversing with you, whether you are male or female. It's a sign that the person likes you. Most people in larger cities have had sufficient contact with Western women to know that they do not appreciate having a stranger grab their breasts. It's perfectly acceptable to remove the hand.

• Expect people to be short-tempered in the summer months (November through March) because of the intense heat.

TELEPHONES

• "Hello" is the standard greeting on the telephone.
• Most operators speak English.
• Look for public telephones around post offices in all major towns and cities.
• Direct dialing is available to most places within Botswana.

• International calls go through an operator. From a public phone, you'll need "tons" of change. In Gaborone, there's a telephone office in the Standard Bank Building on the Mall where you can make long-distance calls. However, the wait may be long. In Francistown, there's a telecommunications office open only during normal business hours. To make a call, pay in advance and go to the assigned booth.

• If you make a call from a private phone, ask for charges so that you can repay your host. When you've completed your conversation, the operator will call with the amount. People are charged even for local calls.

• Keep in mind that in rural areas police stations have radios for use in an emergency.

IN PUBLIC

• Don't be surprised to see good friends—men and men and

women and women—holding hands in public. However, friends of the opposite sex should not indulge in demonstrative behavior (holding hands or kissing) in public. If a man grabs a woman's hand, he's usually making a pass.

• When taking or accepting objects, present or receive them with both hands. Never accept or give anything with your left hand.

• Don't be shy about indulging in noisy behavior; you'll find it everywhere in Botswana.

• A few unusual customs: (1) Blowing the nose on the ground (people hold one nostril while blowing out the other) is common. (2) A man walking with you may turn to the side of a building and urinate on it. (3) Very small children may squat down anywhere and relieve themselves.

• Don't look anyone directly in the eye; it's considered an insult.

• Don't photograph any government-owned buildings.

• Ask permission before photographing someone. Most people enjoy being photographed. If you have an instant camera and can give someone a copy of her/his photograph, you'll make a true friend.

• Feel free to bargain in open markets but not in supermarkets or stores. People *expect* you to bargain in markets and will think you're an idiot if you don't. (You can also trade blue jeans or T-shirts for crafts.)

• In rural villages, people usually sell crafts they have made. You may want to pay the asking price, since people need the money so badly.

• You'll find Western-style toilets in restaurants in cities.

• Carry toilet paper (or tissues) with you. There *may* be some in the public toilet, but it can be anything from reddish cardboard to blue tissue.

DRESS

• Don't expect to find traditional dress. Botswana is too newly independent to have developed any. Dress tends to be Western in style.

• Men should always wear a shirt, no matter how hot it is.

• In villages women should wear skirts that cover their knees. Arms and shoulders should also be covered. Underarms should not show. In cities, jeans and shorts are acceptable.

• Even for major social events, casual dress is acceptable.

MEALS

Hours and Foods

Breakfast: Sometime between 6:00 A.M. and 10:00 A.M. In villages, people have regular tea, chicory coffee, or *rooibas* tea (an herb tea, which older people often prefer) and sorghum porridge (which has a sour taste) or maize meal porridge (which tastes like Cream of Wheat) with sugar and milk.

City families tend to eat Western-style breakfasts: eggs and toast with coffee or tea.

Lunch: Anytime between 11:00 A.M. and 3:00 P.M. In villages people eat *bogobe* (bo-**ho**-bay), a stiff "porridge" served with a sauce made of cabbage and stewed

meat. To eat it, tear off a piece of *bogobe,* and dip it in the sauce.

In the city, people eat sandwiches, steak, *samosas* (fritters stuffed with vegetables and then deep-fried), meat pie, or chicken with rice or french fries.

Dinner: Sometime between 6:00 and 10:00 P.M. Most people eat steak, since it's plentiful and fairly cheap. The usual side dish is rice. Another common dinner is chicken, served with french fries or rice. The only vegetables served regularly are coleslaw, beets, and carrot salad. For dessert, there's often pudding or cake.

• Tea breaks occur at 10:00 A.M. and 4:00 or 5:00 P.M. Very sweet tea is served with bread and butter or fat cakes (which are like fried dough).

• Don't expect crocodile (a popular dish) to taste like chicken. It tastes like spoiled fish and may make you sick if it's not fresh. If you don't want to try it, tell your host that you have stomach problems.

• Note that the main meat is goat, usually chopped up and served in a sauce.

• Another common food is the mopani worm; the mopani is a caterpillar, which lives in the mopani tree. The worms are cooked in hot ash for 15 minutes, boiled in salt water, or dried in the sun. Dried mopani worms are either deep-fried, roasted, eaten raw, or ground up. One American reported that they taste like cardboard.

• One more staple is *mealie-meal,* a very bland porridge made of maize. Other than at teatime, when it's served thin, it is thickened and served with a sauce and/or mopani worms.

• As in many countries, rice is common.

• In villages everywhere, you'll see merula trees. They produce a small, round, greenish-yellow fruit with a pit in the middle. The fruit is very popular in Botswana.

• Beverages are usually drunk after the meal, not during it.

• You'll find a wide array of beverages available: natural fruit juices from South Africa, sold in major towns and cities; soft drinks, such as Coke, orange soda, ginger beer; teas; coffee; and beer, the drink of preference among Batswana.

• Apart from beer, Botswana's traditional drinks are palm wine; *kgadi* (made from brown sugar and either berries or fungus); and a drink made from fermented merula fruit (tastes like Bailey's Irish Cream).

• If you don't drink, don't worry about being pressured to do so. Nonalcoholic alternatives are al-

ways available, since women rarely drink.

• In villages, older men and women drink home brews: either *bojalwa* (a mild, metallic-tasting alcoholic drink made from sorghum) or *kadi* (another alcoholic drink, made of chewed-up roots with sugar and water, which is then fermented).

• Wine is accepted and is appreciated as a gift by Batswana who are Westernized.

Table Manners

• Expect the family to eat together. (In some countries, men and women dine separately.)

• Be on time to a dinner at someone's home. It's acceptable to be late if you're dining in a restaurant.

• Wait for your host to seat you. Each person has a particular place to sit, depending on social nuances, which may go back several generations.

• At a dinner in a family's home, wait to be served. Only your host and hostess know how many mouths they have to feed. However, at a large party, it's okay to take seconds—and even thirds. There's often a barbecue, called *Braii,* with lots of meat (usually a goat or another animal cooked on a spit). People usually eat the meat with their fingers. Eating as much as is available is a tribute to your host, because it shows him that you are aware that he can afford this luxury.

• Tempting as the aroma of the food may be, never smell it, either while it's cooking or when it's been served. People won't eat the food if you smell it.

• Eat with your right hand, unless someone offers you a spoon (which you should use with your right hand).

• If you are asked to offer a toast, be sure to accept, because you are being honored. Even if you're not asked, offer a toast to someone whose cooperation you are seeking.

• If your plate is empty, and you refuse seconds more than twice, your hosts will usually assume you're finished. If you're full before you've finished, say, "Kay coat-ssay," meaning "I am satisfied" (the "ss" indicates that the second syllable is hissed).

• Smoking after dinner is fine, but don't smoke between courses unless you see Batswana doing it.

• There are no set rules about when to leave after dinner. Sometimes guests leave immediately; at other times they linger for several hours. Much depends on the crowd, how well they know one another, etc. Take your cue from the other guests.

Eating Out

• You'll find many fast-food and take-away restaurants in cities and towns. Many offer chicken, hamburgers, and Indian food.

• Only in Gaborone will you find international restaurants (e.g., Chinese).

• Very few restaurants require reservations. Call and ask.

• Don't expect to find menus posted outside restaurants. There are so few restaurants that everyone in town knows what each serves.

• In most places, a hostess will seat you.

• Diners don't share tables.

• Since the staff will serve you when they feel like it and are adept at ignoring people they consider rude, try starting off with friendly chat with the waiter. It won't hurt to throw in a little flattery about the country, the city, the restaurant, etc.

• Daily specials often include such dishes as goat head or ox tail.

• If you have facilities for cooking (or snacking), visit a supermarket in either Gaborone or

Francistown. Because of the very open trading with South Africa, you'll find great quantities and varieties of food: taco shells, grapefruit, freshly ground coffee, etc. Prices are comparable to those in the U.S. and the United Kingdom.

Specialties

• Some main-course specialties: smoked springbok (an animal similar to an antelope), snake, turtle, crocodile, and goat.

• Everywhere you will find *vetkoek* ("fat cake"), which is similar to fried dough or doughnuts.

HOTELS

• All towns have at least one hotel, and larger towns have several in varying price ranges.

• Expect few vacancies in the best hotels in Gaborone. Rooms are given to expatriate residents who are waiting for permanent accommodation. Unless you've booked through a tour operator, you may have little chance of finding a first-class hotel. The least expensive hotels are likely to be brothels as well.

• The better hotels have private baths, TV, and swimming pools. They may also include an English breakfast in the room rate.

• Several hotels and lodges around the country have camping areas. Most offer facilities for showering, cooking, and washing. Campers may use the hotel bars and restaurants.

• National parks have camping areas, really just places to set up a tent. Toilets may or may not be available.

• If you keep out of sight, you can camp anywhere. However, it's illegal to camp at any place other than the two noted above. If you're detected, seek out the chief of the village or ask at a police station for permission to camp.

• *Never* camp out in a deserted place or by yourself. Any camping out is risky because of the animals. One couple was outside at a camp in sleeping bags and a lion carried off the woman.

TIPPING

- Tipping isn't required, but it's becoming more expected in nicer restaurants and hotels and in taxis. Most places add a 10% service charge. If you want to leave more, an additional 10% would be appropriate.
- Restaurants: Most Batswana do not tip.
- Hotel room attendants: Only in large, better hotels. Leave the equivalent of $1.00 U.S. per day.
- Taxis: As a foreigner, you'll be overcharged, so there's no need to tip.
- Theater ushers: Don't tip.

PRIVATE HOMES

- People drop in unannounced on one another because most homes don't have telephones. In fact, if the door is open, people simply walk in.
- Don't visit during the hot part of the day. On weekends, visit in the morning or late afternoon. During the week, call on people during the early evening.
- Realize that the typical household affords little privacy. Houses are small and accommodate many people. If someone offers to show you her/his home, be interested but not nosy. For example, don't comment on three children sharing one bed, etc. Be sure to offer a compliment on something in the house.
- Note that the entertainment style will be determined by the economic level of your hosts. Parties often feature a *Braii* (beef barbecue).

• If you are staying with a family, include them in your plans, unless they are otherwise occupied.

• Offer to help with chores, unless you're staying with a wealthy family that has household help. Your hosts will probably refuse, but they will appreciate your willingness to help.

• In a city home, expect a bathtub but no hot water supply. Daily baths are the norm. Most Batswana bathe in the morning, sometimes following up with a sponge bath at night.

• Don't be surprised if you find underwear hanging in the bathroom to dry. Batswana wash undergarments daily, and they will think you unhygienic if you don't do the same.

Gifts: Give or accept a gift with both hands.

• Popular gifts are T-shirts with American logos and audiocassettes of reggae or country music. People in villages appreciate inexpensive watches, calculators, and flashlights. For city residents, bring tablecloths and tea set covers.

• Only recently has it become acceptable for women to drink. Many who do are fond of Bailey's Irish Cream. It's a good gift to bring if you're invited to a party.

BUSINESS

Hours

Businesses: Monday through Friday, 8:00 A.M. to 5:00 P.M., with a one- or two-hour closing for lunch (usually 1:00 to 2:00 P.M.).

Government Offices: Monday through Friday, 7:30 A.M. to 12:30 P.M. and 1:45 to 4:30 P.M.

Banks: In major towns: Monday, Tuesday, Thursday, and Friday, 9:00 A.M. to 2:00 P.M.; Wednesday, 8:15 A.M. to noon; and Saturday, 8:15 to 10:45 A.M.

On Saturday, no foreign exchange is available at any bank except the Barclays Bank in the Gaborone Sun Hotel.

Some villages have weekly or twice weekly banking services. For specific days, check at banks in large towns.

Stores: Monday through Friday, 8:00 A.M. to 5:00 P.M., with a one-hour closing for lunch, usually between 1:00 and 2:00 P.M.; Saturday, 7:00 A.M. to noon or 1:00 P.M.; and Sunday, closed.

Shops selling alcohol open at mid-morning and close at exactly 7:00 P.M. After that time, you must go to a hotel or restaurant bar.

• If you want to exchange money at one of the main bank branches in Francistown or Gaborone, queue up well before the bank opens. Your transaction may occupy your entire morning. You will fill out many forms, and there will probably be many Zimbabwean shoppers waiting to change traveler's checks.

Money

• The unit of currency is the Pula (abbreviated "P"); one Pula equals 100 Thebe. (*Pula* means "rain," a commodity so precious that the money was named for it.)
• Coins: 1T, 2T, 5T, 10T, 25T, 50T, P1.
• Notes (Bills): P1, 2, 5, 10, 20, 50.
• Most major credit cards are accepted at hotels and restaurants in larger cities and towns.

• When you leave Botswana, you may take out only P500.

Business Practices

• Sources of business contacts: (1) The Commercial Section of the U.S. Embassy, Canadian Embassy, and British Embassy (in Gaborone) offers general market information and assistance with scheduling appointments. (2) The Trade and Investment Promotion Agency (in Gaborone) provides assistance to U.S. firms seeking business. (3) Botswana Development Corporation, a government office, promotes investment by acting as an investment partner in selected sectors. (4) Botswana Confederation of Commerce, Industry, and Manpower (BOCCIM) is the private sector equivalent of the Chamber of Commerce.
• Avoid planning business trips during the heat of the summer (November through February). Batswana will be lethargic—and so will you. In addition, many businesses take an extended holiday during that period. For moderate weather, visit Botswana during October or March.
• Reconfirm your business appointment a day in advance (if possible, directly with the person with whom you're going to meet).

• Note that major hotels provide shuttle bus service to the downtown area, but traveling between business appointments in Gaborone is often difficult. Consider renting a car or hiring a car and driver.

• In larger towns, you'll find faxes, telexes, computers, and some photocopying services.

• Don't expect business to proceed efficiently. Progress will be very slow. Further, people resist any advice on ways to be more productive. One businessperson said that negotiations proceed "an inch at a time."

• Try to cultivate friendships with the people with whom you'll be doing business.

• Be punctual, though meetings often start late.

• Bring business cards; they will impress Batswana.

• English is the official language of government and business.

• When greeting and departing, shake hands *gently*.

• Remember that Batswana tend to be more reserved and formal than Americans. Wait until your business contact uses your first name before you use his or her first name. However, you'll find most Batswana friendly and well disposed toward Americans.

• If you're searching for conversation topics, note that many businessmen and women, as well as government officials, have visited or studied in the U.S. and enjoy talking about it.

• Don't expect people to discuss their families in a business setting.

• Many mid-level and upper-level business and government people leave Gaborone to spend weekends on their family cattle posts. People will enjoy talking about them, but remember that it's impolite to ask how many cattle a person owns.

• Accept the refreshments offered at the beginning of the meeting. After an exchange of pleasantries, broach the subject of the meeting. If you're dealing with a government minister, he will dismiss you when he has enough information. If you aren't dismissed, look for body language or an indirect verbal cue indicating that your counterpart is finished.

• Use graphics, if possible.

• Don't mistake a Batswana's unassertive attitude for naïveté or lack of interest in your business proposal. In addition, don't be put off by the many interruptions likely to occur. Business meetings are often interrupted by long telephone conversations or by the unannounced appearance of colleagues, who may engage in animated conversation for a time and then leave abruptly. You host will resume the meeting, as though nothing happened.

• Visiting businesswomen should take a lesson from Batswana women. They should impress men with their graciousness (showing that they know their place) and their intelligence (showing that they can be relied on). But they should also be prepared to be stubborn in a gentle way.

HOLIDAYS AND SPECIAL OCCASIONS

• Expect banks, government offices, businesses, and many shops to be closed on these national holidays: New Year's (January 1 and 2); President's Day (July 10 and 11); Botswana Day (September 30 and October 1); Christmas Day and Boxing Day (December 25 and 26).

• The following are also national holidays, falling at varying times in March, April, and May: Good Friday; Easter Saturday, Sunday, and Monday; Ascension Day.

TRANSPORTATION

Public Transportation

• The only city with a public transportation system is Gaborone. Look for white minibuses (known as taxis or combis), which follow set routes. They are cheap and fast. Other minibuses, which leave from the railway station, go to surrounding villages.

• To find one of the few conventional taxis in Botswana, look for their distinctive blue number plates. To hail one on the street, wave your hand vertically, with your palm perpendicular to the ground. Negotiate with the driver for the fare before you get in.

• Between their airports and Gaborone, Francistown, and Selebi-Phikwe, the only transport is the minibuses operated by the large hotels for their guests. Sometimes non-guests can ride in one by tipping the driver several Pula. Airport taxis are extremely rare in Gaborone. When you make your hotel reservation, ask that the hotel van meet your flight.

• In the minivans (shared taxis), you'll pay extra for luggage.

• Buses are crowded, usually delayed, and extremely slow. Most leave from the train station.

• Buy a train ticket before boarding. The penalty for not having a ticket is small, but trains are often sold out, so it's a good idea to have your ticket when you get on.

• Expect a lot of rowdiness, smoking, and drinking during train trips. You'll find rows of comfortable seats in first class, while second class, crowded and dirty, has just two benches in each car.

• Usually you can rent an entire cabin in first class, but sometimes other people will be put in with you.

• For overnight travel, first class offers wooden bunks and sinks. Bedding is available for rent. On most journeys, there will be a dining car with overpriced but decent food. The bar will be open for many hours. At some stops, people will sell food and drink that you can buy out of your cabin window. (Be cautious about what you purchase from these vendors.)

• A man and a woman who are traveling together but aren't married should consider using the same last name with the railroad personnel. Otherwise they will try to put you in separate cabins.

• Bring your own water and toilet paper or tissues when traveling by train.

Driving

• Driving is on the left, as in England.

• Botswana has two car rental agencies—Avis and Holiday Car Hire—each with several branches. However, it is probably better to hire a car and driver than to rent a car and drive yourself. Many Batswana drive carelessly, and, more often than not, drink a great deal and drive. In some areas there are no streetlights and no guardrails along the side of the road. Exercise *extreme* caution when either driving or walking.

• Seat belts are compulsory, but there are no special seating rules for children.

• Parking is chaotic, and horn blowing is common.

• Don't drive fast, especially at night.

• Be alert for the many farm animals along the roads, especially when driving through open range.

• If you hit someone's cow, and it survives, the owners are technically responsible for paying you for damages; however, no one is likely to claim the cow.

• Keep in mind that the national speed limit on tarred roads is 110 kph (about 65 mph). Speeds will be posted in towns and villages. If there is no sign, the speed limit is 60 kph (about 35 mph).

• To hire a car or four-wheel-drive vehicle, you must be at least 25 years old and have a driver's license from your own country.

• Obtain a map at a gas station, because it isn't easy to find your way around.

• If you're driving into the Kalahari, be sure to leave your itinerary with someone.

• Should you plan to drive in the bush, where you'll find a series of tracks and ruts, exercise these precautions: (1) Take a good set of maps. (2) Since tracks change frequently, ask directions locally. (3) Carry a compass. (4) Take a 150-litre reserve fuel tank. (5) Take 5 liters of water per person per day. (6) Take spare parts for vehicles. (7) Take a tent and a warm sleeping bag, because the Kalahari can get very cold at night. (8) When driving on sand, consider going in the morning or evening when it will be easier to drive on sand, and lower your tire pressure.

• Expect to encounter roadblocks, where police may ask to search your luggage. Never antagonize these Botswana Defense Force (BDF) soldiers. In the past some have become "trigger happy" with their machine guns.

• Never blow your horn at a herd of elephants. The sound is like that of a baby elephant in distress, and the herd will stampede.

• Keep in mind that fines for foreigners are stiff. You don't pay a fine on the spot. Police give you a ticket, and you'll have to go downtown to pay.

LEGAL MATTERS, SAFETY, AND HEALTH

• Avoid the State House in Gaborone at all times. The BDF will regard you as a trespasser. Further, don't drive down Notwane Road, which leads to the old Gaborone airport; it is now a BDF base.

• Compared to other African countries, Botswana has a very low crime rate. However, there are professional pickpockets, so a money belt is a good idea. What crime there is is not violent.

• When you're walking, be alert for the many unleashed dogs.

• Don't walk close to rivers. The crocodiles are deadly.

• It's relatively safe to hitchhike, if you travel in pairs. Your main risks will be the driver's high speed and level of intoxication.

• Botswana has no drinking age regulation; however, if you're a student—no matter what your age—you may not drink.

• Note that drugs that are illegal in the U.S. are also illegal in Botswana. A local drug called Mandrax is also illegal.

• Expect Customs officers at the airports to be polite but thorough. At the borders, Customs officers can be difficult, depending on their mood. They can and will refuse entry for any reason at all. *Never* show anger, no matter what they do. Try using flattery about the country, your eagerness to visit it, etc.

• Women should expect comments from men on the street, but the likelihood of any physical harassment is very, very slim. However, women should not walk alone at night.

• Remember the standard cautions about food and water: (1) Don't drink tap water, and don't use ice in your drinks. (2) Don't eat raw fruits and vegetables that can't be peeled. (3) Eat only well-cooked meat.

CAMEROON

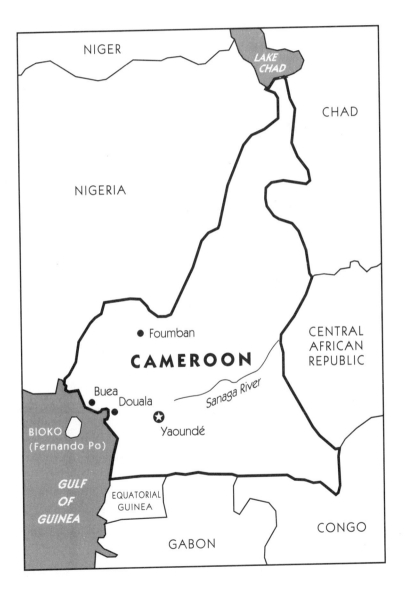

Tucked away in a corner of West Africa, Cameroon could easily be overlooked. However, the country is worth exploration for its fascinating mix of cultures—African traditions blended with reminders of the British and French influence.

Cameroon offers many varieties of natural wonders—tropical forests, beaches, and mountains, with special opportunities to see wildlife in Benoue National Park and Waza National Park.

The French-speaking section of the country is referred to as Francophone, while the English-speaking area is referred to as Anglophone.

GREETINGS

• Always shake hands when greeting and departing, but note that some Muslim men refuse to shake hands with women.

• Be sure to shake hands with *everyone* and introduce yourself when you enter a home. If you don't, you've been very rude.

• Introduce yourself to everyone if you go into an off-license (a bar). People there may ask you very forward questions. For example, if you are white, they may say, "You are white. You are in Cameroon. What are you doing here?"

• Notice a different handshake used by older men. They may hold the right hand to the heart, shake hands, hold the right hand to the heart, and shake hands again. Though it's a traditional form of greeting, foreigners are not expected to use it.

• If you and a Cameroonian are getting on well, expect a special kind of informal handshake. Shake hands, and, as you pull your hand back, snap the other person's middle finger with your thumb. Both people do this simultaneously.

• In the Anglophone section, use the titles "Mr.," "Mrs.," "Miss," "Doctor," "Mayor," and "Professor."

• The following titles of respect are used in Francophone areas: Docteur (for a medical doctor); Monsieur le maire (mayor); Professeur (professor or teacher); Monsieur le Directeur (for the principal of a school; principals are appointed by the President of

Cameroon and have the status of governors); and *Fon* or Chief, for the chief of a tribe.

• In French-speaking sections, the appropriate titles are "Monsieur," "Madame," and "Mademoiselle" with the first name. Anyone woman over 25 will be called "Madame," unless the Cameroonian knows she isn't married.

• Note that in the Anglophone section, "You are there!" is a common greeting, the equivalent of "Hello." In departing, people often say "I'm coming," meaning "I'm leaving."

• Be prepared for first names to be used very soon after you meet someone.

CONVERSATION

• Note that French and English are the official languages of Cameroon, but English is spoken only in larger communities in the far west, bordering Nigeria. Educated people usually speak French.

• With so many groups in rural areas speaking completely different languages, a single trade language was necessary. That language is Fulani.

• Expect women to look down when talking to another person, even to another woman. They never look anyone else in the eye.

• Be prepared for conversation to be accompanied by beer drinking. If you don't want to drink beer, ask for something else. (One traveler was offered a beer in a business setting at 10:00 A.M.)

• When opening a conversation, *always* ask about the man or woman's family, household, health, children—an interchange that can go on for a *long* time.

• Expect to be asked if you are married, have children, etc.

• Cameroonians refer to any slow Western music as "blues." Even Kenny Rogers would be regarded as a blues singer.

• Don't discuss government or politics, because you won't know if people are for or against the government. In the past, people have disappeared for making critical comments about government leaders.

• Don't joke about people who are physically challenged or mentally impaired. Cameroonians think it rude to laugh at a handicapped person. (People with handicaps are not ostracized as they are in much of the West. They often try to do a great deal for themselves—e.g., a woman who was born with no legs and one arm ran a bar and served people.)

• In general, joking and teasing help you to get close to Cameroonians.

• Never speak to a woman— even a close friend—about being pregnant, because women in Cameroon are very superstitious about pregnancy. Avoid such questions as, "When is your baby due?"

• Remember that the term "bush" means out in the middle of nowhere. *Never* use the term, because Cameroonians will be insulted. Instead refer to a place being "in the country."

TELEPHONES

• Don't look for public phones on the street. There aren't any. In Douala the post office has many booths for international calls. All cities have post offices from which you can make long-distance calls. Major hotels in cities have phones and telex facilities. Yaoundé's international telex center (Intelcam) is very efficient.

• Realize that it may take 30 minutes to an hour to make a call out of the country; on the other hand, you may be connected immediately.

• Keep in mind that you can't make collect calls, but at the Intelcam in Yaoundé (the capital), you can call out of the country, give your number, and have the other party call you back.

IN PUBLIC

• One traveler said, "Cameroon is a block party that does not stop." Even though any displays of affection in public are forbidden (*never* kiss or hug in public), illicit activity may go on behind closed doors all night.

• Be prepared for people to tell you what they think you want to hear in order to please you. Example: A Peace Corps volunteer traveled several hours to visit a friend. He wasn't home, but his neighbor said, "He'll be back shortly," even though the neighbor knew that the friend was away for a week. Only through lengthy conversation did the Peace Corps volunteer learn the truth.

• If you can't find a street in a village, just ask someone on the street or in an off-license how to find the person you're looking for. Cameroon is such a social country that everyone knows everyone else. Often people will take you

to the place that you're seeking.

• In the Muslim north, remember these customs: (1) If you visit a mosque, remove your shoes. (2) Some mosques don't admit women, while others have separate entrances for men and women, since the two sexes pray separately. (3) Don't show the soles of your feet.

• Note the two definitions of time: (1) "white man time" means "on time"; (2) "black man time" means one to two hours late or more.

• Be aware of the different attitudes to begging: In the cities, people beg, but in villages people don't because they would be ostracized.

• If you're going to be taking photographs, bring a zoom lens, if possible, so that you can be discreet.

• Respect the rights of those people who refuse to be photographed because they are afraid that their soul will be taken away.

• At most tourist sights, people will ask to be paid to be photographed. They may ask for money, even if you're only photographing crafts in a market. Try bargaining, if you don't want to pay what they've asked.

• In other cases, people may expect a copy of the photo. If you aren't using a Polaroid or other instant camera, take names and addresses—and *be sure* to follow through on sending the photo.

• Recall that photography permits are required only for specialized events such as national or other festivals. However, policemen may stop you and ask for an authorization; possibly they merely want a bribe. Be conscious of who is watching you when you take pictures. Police in cities and towns may confiscate your camera.

• To avoid problems, go to the Ministry of Information in Yaoundé, the capital, where you can obtain a statement that you don't need a permit to take pictures.

• Even if you have a permit, be *very* careful not to photograph any of the following: presidential palaces, airports, military areas and installations, members of the Security and Armed Forces in uniform, bridges, public works sites, airports, post offices, railway stations, harbors—or scenes that could detract from the good reputation of the country.

• People who make more money are expected to pay more in markets. A doctor was charged more for pineapples than a Peace Corps volunteer, and when the volunteer asked why, he was told that the doctor made more money, so he had to pay more. Poor people are often given things for free.

• Don't look for public bathrooms. You will find public facilities only in hotels, where toilets will be Western style. European-style restaurants will probably have a squat toilet; other restaurants and off-licenses may have an outhouse. Toilets are unisex. Carry toilet paper or tissues, because you won't find any.

DRESS

• Keep in mind that even the poorest people dress as well as possible, with well-ironed clothing and polished shoes. Dressing well is a sign of respect. Be sure to wear clean, well-pressed clothing, especially when you're invited to a home.

• For casual wear, women should wear loose summer dresses or cotton pants. Tops could have short sleeves but should not be sleeveless. Men should wear long pants and a shirt.

• Don't wear tribal dress. People in the over 240 tribes in Cameroon are possessive about their costume. Usually, local women wear a *pagne*, a cloth wrapped around the waist and extending to the ankle, sometimes worn with a T-shirt on top and a scarf on the head. Men wear a *boubou*, a long cotton dress worn over matching drawstring pants.

• Don't wear shorts, except when playing sports.

• Never wear torn, dirty jeans or ripped clothes. No matter how poor they are, Cameroonians always look neat and clean.

• If it's hot, an acceptable costume for men is the African suit, also called an "up and down." The suit has pants with a matching long- or short-sleeved shirt, which is more fitted than a regular shirt and is worn outside the pants. Men may wear this outfit for business, if the fabric of the suit is of high quality.

• Never wear camouflage or military clothing, because people may suspect you of being a mercenary.

MEALS

Hours and Foods

Breakfast: In a city, about 7:00 or 7:30 A.M. What people eat depends on their income. In the city, the meal may feature pancakes or fried potatoes and scrambled eggs with bread and margarine. A lighter breakfast might consist of *café au lait* and bread or porridge or *beignets,* which are like doughnuts and in Cameroon would be made with corn flour. In villages, people usually have smoked or dried fish. In areas where tea is grown, people will drink it—one of the popular versions is one made from herbs. Many Cameroonians are also fond of Ovaltine. Those who prefer coffee drink Nescafé mixed with very sweet condensed milk.

Lunch: In a village, about noon. Rice with sauce makes up the meal. In cities, about 1:00 P.M.

Some options are bean stew (called simply "stew"), *fufu* (see "dinner" below), soup, and fried, boiled, or roasted plantains.

Dinner: About 7:00 or 8:00 P.M. If you're invited as a guest, dinner will probably be at 8:00 or 8:30 P.M. Foods may be the same as those at lunch, or there might be either rice with sauce or *couscous,* made with millet or corn.

• In cities, fruit may be served after the meal, but it is more usually served as a snack. Desserts aren't common.

• The popular dish *fufu* can be made of pounded corn or plantains or cocoyams. It has the consistency of very thick porridge. Make a ball of it with your right hand. Then make a depression with your thumb, and scoop up soup, fish, or vegetables into that depression. Pop the *fufu* in your mouth. You are supposed to swallow it whole, not chew it.

• Note that rich people eat chicken; poor people eat beef. In the north, where beef is readily available and common, it's used a great deal in sauces over rice.

• Don't expect pork to be served in Muslim areas.

• In cities, water, wine, beer, or soda (called "a sweet") are drunk with meals. In villages, people usually drink water with the meal

and beer afterward. Among Muslims, Fanta or tea are the standard beverages. As a foreign guest, you may be offered a drink before dinner and probably beer, soda, or water during the meal.

• Many people drink whiskey, or a "moonshine" variant called *Afofo.*

• If coffee is served, it's usually Nescafé.

• Expect *very* strong tea to be drunk by the tribes in the north.

• You may be offered palm wine. When it's new, it's sweet. The longer it ages (possibly just three days) the stronger it becomes. It's safe to drink palm wine, but never drink home-brewed corn vodka. It tastes like rubbing alcohol and can cause blindness. Just plead stomach trouble if it is offered.

• Beverages available in villages are usually beer, soda, or palm wine.

• In English-speaking areas, if beer is offered, and you don't want it, say, "I'll take a sweet." You'll then get a soft drink.

Table Manners

• Realize that in traditional homes men eat first, women next, and children last. A foreign woman visitor will probably eat with the men because she will have a higher status than local women.

• Expect to be served by the women, who will make sure there's enough food for everyone.

• Look for a large bowl on a low coffee table in the living room. Serve yourself with a spoon, putting the food onto your individual plate. Some people eat with the right hand, but as a guest, you will be given a fork or a spoon. However, in some families, everyone eats from individual plates.

• Note that certain foods convey a certain status—e.g., chicken gizzards. As the visitor, you'll be considered the person of status and will be offered the chicken gizzard. If you don't want to eat it, say, "Thank you very much, but I feel that there's someone more deserving than I." Then give the food to the oldest person at the table.

• Every Cameroonian from age six on knows that he may be called on to make a toast and a speech at any time—and they're very good at toasting. A 15-minute speech is not unusual. As a foreigner, you will probably be asked to offer a toast; even if you're not, it's polite to stand and offer a toast—especially if you're an honored guest.

• Don't directly refuse any food offered to you; if you don't want what is presented, ask for a sub-stitute—e.g., a soda instead of a beer.

• A good expression to learn: *Ç'est mon habitude* (meaning "It's my custom"). Use it if you can't or don't want to eat something. Your hosts will understand and won't be offended.

• In the Muslim area in the north, don't drink alcohol in the presence of a Muslim unless he drinks also.

• To follow local custom, smoke only in the evening, after dinner.

• If you're invited to dinner, plan to spend the entire evening with your hosts. Stay at least one to two hours after you've finished the meal.

Eating Out

• In Yaoundé, the capital, you'll find French, Italian, Tunisian, Lebanese, and Asian restaurants. Douala also has a number of ethnic restaurants.

• Keep in mind these distinctions: In the French section of the country, bars are called *bars licenciés*; in English-speaking areas, a bar is a place where there is dancing. A bar as we know it is called an off-license, where the only alcohol served is beer.

• At better restaurants, you'll have a table to yourself. In chop houses, small restaurants with benches, found in villages, sit anywhere, and always talk to the people next to you. Otherwise, you'll be considered rude. Usually, the customers in chop houses are men; a foreign woman should go there with someone.

• To summon the waiter, either hiss (the local custom) or say, "Excuse me." Don't call out "Garçon" or "Boy."

• If you see "bush meat" on the menu, the term refers to anything a hunter shoots—e.g., antelope or monkey.

• If you suggest to someone that he or she join you for a meal, *you* pay. If the other person suggests the meal, let her/him pay. (A Cameroonian woman would probably invite you to a meal in her home, but groups of women—e.g., a group of teachers—may dine out together.)

• In markets, you can get grilled mackerel and sauce or *soya,* which is like beef shish kebab. Be sure that the *soya* is hot in temperature. If it isn't, it's been standing around for a long time.

• In villages, in little restaurants attached to homes, you can order skewers of meat with french fries and beer.

• At the roadside, you'll find women selling grilled fish with a spicy dressing. Be sure the fish is hot in temperature.

Specialties

• Here are some of Cameroon's special foods: *koki*—black-eyed peas with spinach, palm oil, and spices in the form of a cake, eaten with boiled green plantains; stew—fresh tomatoes with garlic, ginger, and vegetable oil eaten with rice, potatoes, plantains, or yams (which are not like American yams but are a root like cassava); *jammu-jammu*—a thick, slimy stew of spiced spinach-like leaves served with *fufu,* and, if the family is rich, a bit of meat (scoop out a ball of *fufu* with your right hand, and dip it into the *jammu-jammu*).

• *Piment,* a hot oily pepper sauce that looks like salad dressing, is always served with meals.

• In the northwest, try a dish called *achu,* which is made of pounded cocoyam and filled with palm oil, ashes, limestone, and hot pepper. The porridge-like substance is formed into a mound, with a crater in the middle. Take one finger, scoop up the cocoyam, and dip it in the sauce in the crater. Don't spoil the crater so that the sauce runs out.

HOTELS

TIPPING

• Be aware that hotels are either at the high end or the low end of the comfort/amenities scale. There is little in between.

• At major hotels guests are served a continental breakfast; it's included in the room rate.

• Be prepared to surrender your passport for 24 hours while the hotel staff registers you with the police.

• Don't expect to find hotels in small towns. Ask at a restaurant if there are rooms for rent there or if the staff knows of someone who rents.

• At a restaurant, check to see if service is included in the bill. If not, at better and medium-priced restaurants, leave a tip of 10%.

• If you ask a child to do a chore for you, give her/him the equivalent of 15 to 25 cents U.S.

• Don't tip taxi drivers.

• At a hotel, give a person who calls a taxi for you the equivalent of 50 cents to $1.00 U.S.

• In the Anglophone section, the word "dash" is used loosely to mean a tip or a bribe.

PRIVATE HOMES

• Don't feel you have to phone ahead before visiting, primarily because most people don't have phones. Even if they do, you need not call in advance.

• Note that people often drop in at mealtimes.

• If you're invited to visit at a specific time, arrive 15 to 30 minutes late.

• When you first visit people, expect them immediately to take out their photo album to show you their family pictures.

• In a village in Anglophone Cameroon, after you have been served a meal, the hosts will "open the floor" for dancing. A master of ceremonies will pair off people for the first dance—e.g., the mayor will dance with the doctor's wife; the doctor will dance with the mayor's wife. After the first dance, everyone enters the dancing.

• Don't be surprised to find a man living hours away from home because of his work. His wife and children remain on the tribal land. Cameroonians find it odd that when Americans move for work the entire family moves.

• A Cameroonian saying—"A man is not a turtle; he doesn't travel with his house on his back"—means that when you visit, people must extend hospitality to you (i.e., offer to put you up for the night). If you're stranded in a village, a local family will usually take you in, if you ask, because it's traditional to take in strangers who have no place to stay.

• If you're a man staying in a village, you may be asked if you want a blanket. Your host is really asking if you want a woman to sleep with. Make it clear that you really want a blanket!

• Note that people wash frequently. Since rarely is there hot water, people in villages heat pots of water or bathe in streams or lakes. In lakes and streams, women and men wash in separate areas.

• Your hosts will not expect you to help with household chores. However, if you stay with a family, be prepared to contribute food or to buy gas for a boat, if the family men are fishermen.

• Don't be surprised if village children follow you everywhere. They are very curious.

Gifts: If invited to a meal, bring whiskey, wine, or whatever fruit is in season.

• From abroad, bring any of the clothing, following if the family has children: clothing, toys, soccer balls, volleyballs, school supplies, audio cassettes (country singers Don Williams and Kenny Rogers are both popular).

• People of all ages appreciate anything American—e.g., jeans, T-shirts.

• Men *and* women in villages enjoy pipes.

• If someone has a VCR that will play American tapes, bring videos.

BUSINESS

Hours

Businesses: Monday through Friday, 8:00 A.M. to noon and 2:30 to 5:30 P.M., and Saturday, 8:00 A.M. to 1:00 P.M.

Government Offices: Monday through Friday, 8:00 A.M. to noon and 2:30 to 5:30 P.M., and Saturday, 8:00 A.M. to 1:00 P.M.

Banks: Monday through Friday, 8:30 to 11:45 A.M. and 2:45 to 4:15 P.M.; closed Saturday.

Stores: Monday through Saturday, 9:00 A.M. to 12:30 P.M. and 4:00 to 7:00 P.M.

Money

• The unit of currency is the Central African Franc, abbreviated CFA. It's pegged to the French franc, so you'll be able to convert unused currency into French francs.

• Coins: 1, 5, 10, 25, 50, 100, and 500 francs.

• Notes (Bills): 1,000, 5,000, and 10,000 francs.

• In Yaoundé and Douala, you may use your credit cards in hotels, airports, and for car rentals.

• In street markets, there is a black market for exchanging currency. Best to avoid it.

Business Practices

• Consider joining the Lions Club before you leave North

America. You'll be able to go to the Cameroon meetings, where you'll have good opportunities for networking. You'll then find other business organizations in Cameroon that will be excellent sources of contacts. Another source for business is the Chamber of Commerce in Douala.

• Send a fax a month in advance to make an appointment. Allow even more time if you're planning to meet with a government minister.

• Avoid making appointments in May because there are several holidays during that month. During May, no one works more than about a week.

• If you're writing to a business in the Anglophone area, you can use the same style letter as you would at home. However, in the Francophone area, be very formal and flowery.

• In the Francophone section, most people speak English; however, they will appreciate it if you learn some French.

• Be punctual, but don't be surprised if Cameroonians are 30 minutes to an hour late. There are often problems with transportation.

• Expect Cameroonians to be very open to new goods and new business initiatives.

• Prepare for a brief initial period of conversation, but people

then will get right down to business. Cameroonians believe that they'll come to know you through discussing business. However, businessmen will be very cautious until they feel completely comfortable with you.

• Keep in mind that people will tell you what they think you want to hear. Should you ask, "Can you deliver 2,000 widgets by June 1?" the response will be "Yes," whether or not the delivery is possible. Ask a less direct question: "When do you think you could deliver 2,000 widgets?" Continue to probe to be sure you're getting the truth.

• Realize that there are bureaucratic hurdles. One way to surmount them is to give "tips." These "tips" aren't really bribes. In Cameroon it is customary to bring a gift, a goat, or a drink to the chief when asking for a favor. Money has taken the place of gifts, and the habit of such gifts has spread into other sectors.

• Cameroonian businessmen appreciate receiving gifts, and they will offer you gifts when you have proved yourself trustworthy and have developed a relationship with them. You will usually be presented with Cameroonian artwork.

• From North America, bring personal pocket calendars, computerized phone directories, or other small electronic gadgets.

• In the Anglophone section, don't be surprised to be invited to a late business lunch—4:00 P.M. isn't unusual. In the Francophone section, business dinners starting at 8:00 P.M. are common.

• Note that Cameroonians will probably treat foreign business-people at restaurants called chicken *parlows,* where barbecued chicken or grilled fish are featured.

• If you wish to entertain a Cameroonian, take him to any of the wide variety of restaurants available—French, Italian, Chinese, and African.

tional Day (May 20); Feast of the Assumption (August 15); Christmas (December 25).

• The following days are observed in accordance with the Muslim calendar: Ramadan; the end of Ramadan celebration; the Festival of Sacrifices (69 days after Ramadan).

• A *Cry Die* is a celebration of a person's life after he/she has died. The commemoration may take place even five years after the death, because it costs a great deal of money for food, drink, etc. A *Cry Die* is a public event, so participate—eat, drink, and dance—if you see one. It's customary to bring whiskey, wine, or beer to help the family defray expenses.

HOLIDAYS AND SPECIAL OCCASIONS

• The following holidays are observed in Cameroon: New Year's Day (January 1); Youth Day (February 11); Labor Day (May 1); Na-

TRANSPORTATION

Public Transportation

• Note that public transportation is well organized. Notices stating the official fare (CFA per kilometer) are posted in every vehicle. However, baggage charges are not fixed. Try bargaining with drivers about baggage costs, but you're really at their mercy.

• Shared taxis (also called "bush taxis") are the major means of public transportation. Front seats are considered the most desirable, but you may have three or four people crushed in on top of you, if you're one of the first to arrive.

• Banging on the side of a shared taxi means "Go." To signal it to stop when you want to get out, yell "Stop."

• For a long-distance taxi, go to a taxi park. (You'll also always find food and drink there.) You can't really plan your departure time, since the taxis don't leave until they're full. As a rule, people tend to travel early in the day, because it's cooler.

• If you're traveling a long distance and need to change shared taxis, make sure to have someone map out your route in advance. Very often, the driver of the first taxi will not know how to get to the village where you will need to make the change.

• A train, called a *couchette,* links north and south Cameroon. On these overnight trains, first class offers a *couchette,* with four to a compartment, a restaurant, and air-conditioning. The *couchettes* are made up into beds. Make sure to use the toilets early, or they won't be clean. Second class is packed with people, who often bring with them goats and chickens. (Note that the term *couchette* refers to the train, the compartment, and the sleeping accommodations.)

• In sleeper cars, the staff may put people in the aisle; if you have to use the bathroom, be prepared to trip over people sleeping on the floor.

• Note that the night train is an express, while the day train is *very* slow. At stops along the way, you can buy food and drink from the people who will bring them to the window.

• Be careful at the airport, because people will try to grab your bags to get a tip.

Driving

• If you plan to drive outside a city, you may have a problem renting a car.

• An American driver's license is acceptable for renting a car.

• *However,* it is far better to rent a car with a driver. Should you be involved in an accident, you *don't want* to be the driver. Another reason not to drive yourself is that many people drive very fast with brakes and lights that don't work—and the drivers are often drunk.

- In cities, parking is a major problem. There are no garages (and no meters).

- If you hire a driver or a guide in the north (the Muslim area), he may need to stop to pray five times a day.

LEGAL MATTERS, HEALTH, AND SAFETY

- Realize that there are checkpoints with armed police at roads all around the country. You will invariably be stopped and asked for your papers. Sometimes the police are looking for a bribe. They may, for example, say that you need a certain sticker, which you don't know about and which probably doesn't exist. If you chat and act friendly, you may avoid paying the bribe. However, if you argue, you may be detained for hours. If you have to bribe, give 1,000 to 2,000 francs, and say, "It's so hot; use this to buy yourself a beer."

- If you're feeling strong, you can try to intimidate the police. Example: Police stopped a taxi driver whose American passenger had a seven-foot-long fishing rod in a case that was sticking out the window. The policeman opened the case. When the American asked for his name and badge number, the policeman told them to drive on.

- When you arrive in a new area and are going to be there for a while, always register with the police. Also, seek out the mayor. Since the war with Chad and Libya, people are suspicious of strangers.

- Note that violent crime is almost nonexistent. The most common crime is theft.

- Never trust people at a train station who offer to help you find your seat and try to take your bag. Bag snatching is on the increase.

- Beware of pickpockets, but realize that merchants and vendors in markets will be protective. Example: A foreign woman had her pocket picked in a market. People in the market chased the children who did it for a full hour and finally caught them. The children were then taken to the police station and beaten. The foreign woman had to witness the punishment so that she could see that justice was done.

• Be aware that if you have an item that looks as though it's of historical value, you will be stopped when you leave the country. And the Customs officers can be very intimidating. Example: An American who was leaving the country had his bags checked by Customs agents who discovered antelope horns that had been given to the American as a gift. The Customs officials told him that he needed a sticker, which could be obtained only in the city. The American replied that a very important person, Monsieur le Député, had given him this gift. Unimpressed, the Customs officer told him to get a taxi into town and advised him how much the fare would be. The American said, "I'll give you the money, and you give me the sticker." His strategy worked.

• When you deal with any officials, be prepared for very aggressive behavior on their part.

• Don't drink tap water. Don't eat fruits or vegetables that aren't peeled, and don't buy food from street vendors unless the temperature of the food is hot.

• Keep in mind that people use the edges of lakes and streams as bathrooms. Don't swim in them for that reason and also to prevent contracting the parasitic disease bilharzia.

• Women should keep in mind that they are more likely to be harassed in the south of Cameroon than in the north.

• A final note on race relations: Cameroonians like Americans, but they're not very fond of the French. African-Americans may be treated differently from white Americans because Cameroonians don't understand why African-Americans don't behave as Cameroonians do. Example: An African-American woman was asked to carry jugs of water on her head and pound corn with the women, while a white American female was not expected to do the same.

KEY PHRASES

English	French Pronunciation
Good day	bawn-**zhoor**
Good evening	bawn-**swahr**
Please	seel-voo-**pleh**
Thank you	mehr-**see**
You're welcome	de ree-en
Yes	wee
No	nawn
Mr., Sir	meh-**syeu**
Mrs., Madame	mah-**dahm**
Miss	mahd-mwah-**zehl**
Excuse me	ex-kyou-zay **mwah**
Good-bye	o reh-**vwahr**
I don't understand	zhe ne kawn-prahn **pah**
I don't speak French	zhe ne pahrl pah frawn-**seh**
Do you speak English?	pahr-lay voo ahn-**gleh**?

COTE D'IVOIRE

(IVORY COAST)

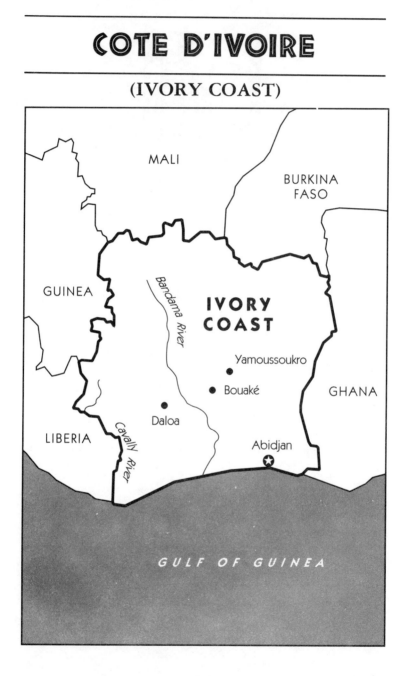

Ice skating in Africa? The largest Roman Catholic basilica after St. Peter's in Rome? A tropical rain forest? Find all three in the Côte d'Ivoire. The Hôtel Ivoire boasts an ice rink; the basilica, "Our Lady of Peace," in Yamoussoukro accommodates 7,000 worshipers; and the tropical rain forests are classified as world reserves by UNESCO.

For a special experience, watch the Banco laundrymen in the most amazing display of organized chaos as they beat clothing on rocks strewn in the Banco River.

There is a noticeable difference in climate in the two sections of the country. Humidity is close to 100% around Abidjan, but it's as low as 15% in the north at the height of the dry season.

GREETINGS

CONVERSATION

- Always shake hands when greeting. Men and men shake hands, as do men and women, and women and women.
- If you're introduced to a group, wait for others to extend their hands.
- Be sure that your handshake is firm.
- Note that it's important to use titles. They can be used with or without the person's name. Titles: Professeur; Directeur (for the director of an organization); Docteur; Chef (for a village chief).

- Most people speak some French.
- Don't ask many questions initially. Just tell others who you are, what you do, and why you are visiting the Ivory Coast; then allow others to tell you about themselves.
- Always inquire about how a person's family is—wife and children. In the north, people will ask about parents, sisters, cousins, etc. In the middle section of the country, it's not so important to inquire about each relative individually.

• Don't ask people about their political affiliations, their opinion of the former president, or their political views in general.

• Don't be surprised if people are aggressive in conversation.

TELEPHONES

• Note that you can buy telephone cards at the post office; however, most public phones don't work, and sometimes the cards don't work. For safety's sake, don't make lengthy calls from a public phone. Someone may accost you in the booth and rob you.

• Service is better for local calls than for international calls.

• International operators speak English.

• In Abidjan, make calls or send faxes from the post office or the Hôtel Ivoire, which has a communications center.

IN PUBLIC

• Avoid brusque, flamboyant body movements. (For example, if you're excited, don't flail your arms around.) Ivorians are guarded in their gestures.

• Don't be surprised if people hiss to attract another person's attention outdoors (e.g., in a market).

• The gesture associated with no is *not* shaking the head. People indicate the negative by clicking the upper teeth with the tongue.

• If you hear the term *Too-bah-boo,* note that an Ivorian is trying to attract the attention of a white person. The word may also be used to call an African-American. The expression is in no way derogatory.

• Outside a home or semi-enclosed area, Ivorians clap their hands two or three times, as a gesture requesting permission to enter. The equivalent of knocking on a door when there is no door, it's an acknowledgment of private space.

• Bargain for everything except food, including food in outdoor markets.

• In cities, don't photograph scenes of abject poverty. You will offend Ivorians.

• In rural areas, where people aren't used to cameras, ask permission before photographing. People will usually ask you to send them a picture. Be sure to do so.

• For public bathrooms, look in hotels and restaurants in cities. They are labeled *Hommes* (Men) and *Femmes* (Women).

• In rural areas, restaurants will have an unmarked outhouse.

• Never show surprise or offense when people urinate in public—a fairly common occurrence.

They dress very formally and are very fashion conscious.

• For casual attire, women may wear loose pants. (Tight pants with shirts tucked into them would be too hot and wouldn't look appropriate.) Consider having African cotton made into a loose dress; many foreign women do, because the dresses are so comfortable in the heat.

• If men don't want to look like tourists, they should avoid wearing shorts, unless they're playing golf or tennis.

• Women should *never* wear shorts, except at beaches. If you wish to wear shorts, bring a wraparound skirt to wear over them.

• For business, men should wear a two- or three-piece suit and tie. Women should wear a dress or a suit.

DRESS

• Notice that Ivorians dress in the French style, even in villages.

MEALS

Hours and Foods

Breakfast: About 7:00 or 8:00 A.M. Ivorians tend to eat left-overs from the night before. As a foreign guest, you will be offered a baguette with butter and jam. Though Ivorians usually drink tea at breakfast, you will be offered coffee.

Lunch: Sometime between noon and 2:00 P.M. The meal may consist of chicken and a sauce, *attiéké,* or *foutou* (see "Specialties" below).

Dinner: Between 8:00 and 9:00 P.M. Foods will be the same as those at lunch.

• Ivorian cooking doesn't vary much. Meals consist of a sauce, based on tomatoes, onions, hot peppers, and other vegetables; this sauce is served with a starch.

If the people can afford it, the sauce will contain chicken or fish.

• In Muslim areas, people usually don't drink alcohol or eat pork. Some Muslims, however, drink in the privacy of their homes.

• Note that coffee is more common than tea. The coffee is always Nescafé with a *great* deal of sweetened condensed milk added. To Western palates, the taste is cloying. Never expect fresh milk in your coffee.

• Don't drink tap water or beverages with ice from local water. You can drink AWA, a brand of bottled water.

Table Manners

• When invited to a meal, arrive about 15 minutes late. Some guests may be as much as 45 minutes late.

• In cities, upper-middle-class families will offer an apéritif before dinner.

• Ask for coffee or tea instead of tap water, which isn't safe to drink.

• Ivorians usually don't drink during a meal, but afterward have soda or water, not hot drinks. However, in the cities, upper-class people have adopted French customs and generally drink red wine with meals; if you don't want to drink alcohol, ask for a soda.

• In villages a foreign woman invited to dinner will probably be seated with the men. Men are served first, women eat the leftovers, and children eat what is left after that.

• Use only the right hand when eating.

• In cities, expect to use utensils and individual plates. In villages, people often eat from a common bowl. A guest may be given a separate bowl and spoon, but people are pleased if you share food from the communal bowl.

• If children are hanging around when men are eating, don't be surprised if the men give the children some food. You can join in this custom if you wish, but wait for your host to make the first move.

• Expect silence during the meal. Ivorians never talk while eating. They eat quickly and then socialize while they are digesting. Some people believe that if you talk while you eat, you might choke.

• As a guest, you are expected to eat a great deal, or your hosts will think that you don't like the food and will be *very* insulted.

• In cities, Ivorians tend to stay up late, so feel free to stay for as long as two hours after dinner. In rural areas, where people rise with the sun, stay only an hour.

Eating Out

• In Abidjan, you'll find French, Italian, Chinese, and Lebanese restaurants, as well as several specializing in seafood.

• *Maquis,* found all over, are cheap, open-air restaurants with chairs and tables. They usually offer only beef brochettes (shish kebab) and braised chicken or fish, served with onions, tomatoes, and *attiéké.* (Avoid raw tomatoes. They aren't safe.)

• If you invite a Muslim to a restaurant, feel free to have an alcoholic beverage yourself, if you wish.

• Be sure to check your bill to make sure you haven't been overcharged.

Specialties

• A special and very common dish is *foutou,* which consists of boiled yams or plantains pounded into a paste of sticky, mashed-potato-like consistency. *Foutou* and rice are usually served with a sauce—e.g., *sauce arachide,* made with peanuts, or *sauce graine,* made with palm oil nuts.

• Two other well-known dishes: *attiéké* (at-chay-kay), grated marioc, which resembles rice; and *kedjenou,* chicken, vegetables, and a mild sauce.

TIPPING

• Note that Africans and French don't tip, but they usually expect tips from foreigners and people using hotels.

• Restaurants: Service is included, but it's customary to leave the equivalent of $1.00 U.S. extra.

• Porters: At the airport, there's a fixed charge. To other porters, give the equivalent of $1.50 U.S.

• Taxis: There isn't a set percentage, but round the fare up. For example, if the fare is 1,375 francs, give the driver 1,500 francs.

• Hotel room attendants: Leave the equivalent of $1.00 U.S. per day.

• Men who guard your parked car: Give the equivalent of 30 cents U.S.

• Young boys who carry your packages for you in markets or supermarkets: Give the equivalent of 30 cents U.S.

• If someone on the hotel staff, such as the concierge, has been especially helpful, tip him or her the equivalent of $3.00 U.S. at the end of the week.

PRIVATE HOMES

• Don't arrange a visit in advance. If you do, people will be offended. People usually visit sometime between 4:00 and 7:00 P.M. If you arrive around 7:00 P.M., your Ivorian friends will expect you to stay to dinner.

• When you visit a home you will be offered soft drinks or liqueurs but not wine. Wine is served only with meals.

• If calling long distance from a home, always call collect.

• Never walk into a kitchen unless you're invited.

• If you visit Muslims during Ramadan, don't eat in front of them (since Muslims will be fasting).

• If staying with a family, try to be as independent as possible. Ask for suggestions about things to see and do, but do your sightseeing on your own.

• Keep your belongings in your room, not spread out throughout the house. It's both a matter of courtesy and safety. You don't know who may be coming through the house, and your property could disappear.

• In upper-class homes, there is usually hot water for baths. If the electricity goes off, the maid will heat some water. Check family schedules to learn who needs the bathroom at what time.

• Never offer to help with chores.

• Don't tip household help in a home.

• If the home you're visiting has a guard at the gate of its parking lot, give him the equivalent of $5.00 U.S. at the end of a week.

Gifts: If invited to a dinner, bring a bottle of gin or champagne, unless your hosts are Muslims. In that case, bring pastries from one of the many French bakeries.

• From abroad, bring *blank* video cassettes. They will work on the VCRs available in the country, but films won't work.

• Small cameras are also a good gift.

BUSINESS

Hours

Businesses: Monday through Friday, 8:00 A.M. to noon and 2:30 to 6:00 P.M., and Saturday, 8:00 A.M. to noon.

Government Offices: Monday through Friday, 7:30 A.M. to noon and 2:30 to 5:30 P.M., and Saturday, 7:30 A.M. to noon.

Banks: Monday through Friday, 7:30 A.M. to noon and 2:00 to 5:00 P.M.; closed Saturday.

Stores: Monday through Saturday, 8:00 A.M. to noon and 3:00 to 7:00 P.M.

Money

• The unit of currency is the West African Franc, abbreviated CFA.
• Coins: 1, 5, 10, 50, 100, and 500 CFA.
• Notes (Bills): 500, 1,000, 2,500, 5,000, and 10,000 CFA. (As the amount increases, the size of the bill grows larger.)
• Credit cards are accepted in hotels and large restaurants. You can also use them to get cash at a bank.

Business Practices

• Good sources of contacts: (1) The Department of Commerce at the U.S. Embassy, Canadian Embassy, or British Embassy is a good first step. (2) The American Chamber of Commerce in Abidjan is another good source for business contacts. The organization meets at the Hôtel Ivoire once a month.
• Many people in banking and business speak English, but most businesspeople have been educated in France. If you aren't fluent in French, hire an interpreter through the U.S. Embassy, Canadian Embassy, or British Embassy or the U.S. Agency for International Development (USAID).

• About a month before your visit, write ahead for an appointment. Call to follow up. Call again with your expected arrival date. Tell people that you'll be in the country for only a week, even if you plan on staying longer. Never let it be known that you have time available, because Ivorians may put off seeing you. If a situation develops where you need to be in the country longer than you first announced, say that you have to call your home office to get permission to extend your stay.
• As soon as you arrive, call to reconfirm your appointments.
• Remember that everything depends on how important your business is to the Ivorians. Your biggest problem may be that a businessperson will show up the first time (often as much as three hours late) but will not show up for a second appointment.
• Don't make appointments during Ramadan. Muslims' abilities will be at a low ebb because they fast during the day. Be especially sure to avoid appointments in the afternoon during Ramadan, because people will be very tired.
• If you want to set up a business, prepare to spend time letting people know who you are, what your family is like, what your plans are, and that you are a person of integrity.

• Note that you'll have access to good business equipment. Fax services as well as computer rentals are available at the best hotels, and photocopying services are everywhere. The university (Université Nationale d'Abidjan) also has a business center, which you can use, but you must make arrangements to do so in advance.

• Business is conducted slowly, though people are very direct initially. Be wary if people try to jump into a final agreement very quickly.

• Expect decisions to be made by people at the top of the organization; however, the people with whom you're dealing may have family connections with the decision makers, which will mean that the deal could be finalized without a great deal of red tape.

• Realize that the system is heavily bureaucratic. Because of devaluation of the CFA and a new regime, efforts are being made to end fraud and the considerable nepotism.

• If your company is going to send a woman to do business, be sure that she has had experience in other foreign countries. It's best to send a married woman, because the married state is respected. Unmarried woman may be the subject of advances by Ivorian businessmen, and the business re-lationship may be jeopardized. In all cases, women should be serious and professional.

• If Ivorians want your business, they may make great efforts to please you by wining and dining you—often in their homes.

• Lunches, which sometimes last for two or three hours, are more popular than dinners for business entertainment.

• If you wish to entertain an Ivorian for business, treat him or her to a meal at a good hotel restaurant.

• Include a spouse in an invitation to a restaurant for dinner, if you've been to the couple's home, the spouse seems interested in her husband's work, and she is educated. Otherwise, she won't feel comfortable. If in doubt, issue the invitation, and the spouse can choose to accept or decline.

• If you develop a business relationship with an Ivorian, you can ask her or him if there is something she or he would like you to bring from abroad—a part for a computer or a piece of software, for example.

HOLIDAYS AND SPECIAL OCCASIONS

• Côte d'Ivoire observes the following holidays: New Year's Day (January 1); Easter Monday; Labor Day (May 1); Feast of the Assumption (August 15); All Saints' Day (November 1); National Day (December 7); Christmas (December 25).

• The following holidays vary according to the Muslim calendar: end of Ramadan; Tabaski.

• Tabaski is the most important holiday for West African Muslims. The day, which commemorates the moment Abraham prepared to sacrifice his son to God, coincides with the end of the *Hajj,* the pilgrimage to Mecca. People slaughter sheep and give one-third to the poor, one-third to friends, and one-third to family. Celebrations center on visiting friends after many hours at the mosque.

TRANSPORTATION

Public Transportation

• Note that hotels have free shuttles to and from the airport. If you send your arrival time in advance, a runner will come to the airport and help you through Customs.

• Be aware that city taxi drivers often rig their meters. Have a member of the hotel staff give you a map, tell you how far the ride should be, and how much it should cost. One method taxi drivers use to overcharge is to take a much longer route than necessary.

• Remember that taxi rates double after midnight.

• After entering a private taxi, put on your seat belt; if you don't and you're caught, you'll be fined.

• Bush taxis run throughout the country. Some are Peugeot 504s, and some are minibuses. If you're concerned that one of the Peugeots will be too crowded for comfort, consider paying for two seats. However, it's better to take one of the large, luxurious buses between cities. They cost about the same as a bush taxi, are much more comfortable, have definite departure times, and offer one seat per person.

• The only train line runs from Abidjan to Ouagadougou and is a way to get to major towns in the interior. Two trains run on this route: (1) *The Gazelle,* which leaves Abidjan daily, features *couchettes* (two persons to a compartment), clean sheets, a dining car, and air-conditioning. Couchettes are often fully booked, but usually not more than a day in advance. (2) *The Express,* which also leaves Abidjan daily, is less expensive, but it is less comfortable. Though it has a dining car, it doesn't have air conditioning, and the *couchettes* accommodate four persons per compartment.

Driving

• If you book your rental car in advance, you'll be met with the car at the airport at Abidjan. The major car rental firms—Hertz, Avis, Budget, and Eurocar—all have branches there.

• Expect to find roads paved and in good condition. However, people drive very fast, and there are many accidents.

• Be sure that everyone in the car is wearing seat belts (if the car has them); you can be fined for not wearing them.

• At night, be alert for the remote possibility of an animal crossing the road.

LEGAL MATTERS, HEALTH, AND SAFETY

• Be sure that you don't bring in any illegal drugs—there are heavy penalties. It's wise to bring any prescription medicine in its original bottle with the contents clearly labeled. If you want to be supercautious, bring a letter from your physician stating what each drug is for.

• Leave all jewelry, watches, purses, and wallets in the hotel safe in Abidjan to protect yourself against the all-too-frequent street crimes. Visitors have reported theft of even very inexpensive watches.

KEY PHRASES

English	*French Pronunciation*
Good day	bawn-**zhoor**
Good evening	bawn-**swahr**
Please	seel-voo-**pleh**
Thank you	mehr-**see**
You're welcome	de ree-en
Yes	wee
No	nawn
Mr., Sir	meh-**syeu**
Mrs., Madam	mah-**dahm**
Miss	mahd-mwah-**zehl**
Excuse me	ex-kyou-zay **mwah**
Good-bye	o reh-**vwahr**
I don't understand	zhe ne kawn-prahn **pah**
I don't speak French	zhe ne pahrl pah frawn-**seh**
Do you speak English?	pahr-lay voo ahn-**gleh**?

GHANA

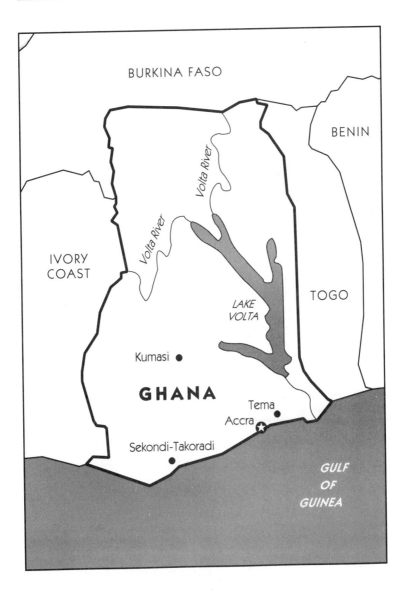

Ghana, the first black African colony to achieve independence (March 6, 1957), includes more than 75 ethnic groups, who are divided between the country's two distinct climates—warm, humid air from the Atlantic in the south and hot, dry air from the Sahara in the north. However, the temperature averages a pleasant 78 degrees F. (26 degrees C.).

Those interested in African art will find a splendid supply of wood carvings, especially masks.

GREETINGS

• In greeting, expect to shake hands with members of both sexes. Men and men, men and women, and women and women shake hands. They grasp right hands, twist and click one another's middle finger while still holding hands, and then let go.

• In villages, people don't shake hands. They touch right cheek, left cheek, and right cheek again (as the French do). Good friends may hug at the same time.

• Use titles: Doctor (for a Ph.D. or an M.D.); Professor; Chief. Refer to men as "Sir" and women as "Madame," except for very young women, who should be called "Miss."

• People have a last name, but you may have to ask what it is. Then use it with one of the above forms of address.

• Don't use first names until you know people well.

• Ghanaians have several names. They sometimes use their Christian name and sometimes they use the day of the week on which they were born as their name. A nurse in the Peace Corps was called Madame (for age and status) Aba-Thursday. (The name of the weekday will be translated into the local language.)

• Always greet the oldest person in a group first.

• Don't use your left hand—even for waving.

• Don't be surprised to see men holding hands or linking little fingers.

• In a village, address any male over 30 (or a male with children) as *pah-pah* with or without the last name. A woman over 30 (or one with children) is *mah-mee* with or without the last name. Call both men and women over 50 *nah-nah,* a term used for anyone to whom one wants to show respect—a chief, an elder, a fetish priest or priestess (whether young or old).

• In Ghana, people do not address men and women of their parents' generation by first names.

CONVERSATION

• Note that English is the official language, but many different languages are used in various areas.

• Be sure to be reserved— never pushy—when you first start conversing with people.

• Don't ask people what *tribe* they belong to. Use the word "group" instead.

• Don't gossip.

• Don't discuss the government.

• Pay sincere compliments. Ghanaians appreciate them.

• Inquire about a Ghanaian's family's health. Ask, "How is your work going?" "Are you planning any trips?" "How is your schooling going?"

• Ask people about their children. They enjoy explaining the origins of their children's names, since each name has a significance.

• If you're speaking to a child, he/she won't look you in the eye, since that would be an act of disrespect.

• If you bring children to Ghana—or are just with a party that includes children—don't be surprised if Ghanaians tease and taunt them.

• Expect to be asked about your family and their health.

• Praise God frequently in conversation; it's a custom in both Christian and Muslim areas.

• Prepare to be asked frequently which church you attend. To avoid offending, you might wish to name a church, even if you don't go to one.

• Don't feel that you have to fill every minute with conversation. Ghanaians are very comfortable with silence.

TELEPHONES

• Don't look for public phones on the street.

• To make an overseas call, go to the post office. Buy a phone card there, and insert it in the phone slot. Special phones at the post office have access to an AT&T international operator. You can also make overseas calls from the better hotels. Before you do, be sure to ask if there's a surcharge. If it's a large one, you'll have to weigh the convenience of calling from your room against the probably long wait at the post office.

• At the P&T (Post & Tele-communication) office, pay, after telling the clerk how long you wish to talk. It's advisable to plan on a little extra time, since there will be very little warning that the call is ending. If you wish, you can call collect from P&T offices.

• You can't make overseas calls from most private homes.

• In Kumasi and Accra, you can make phone calls from communication centers, which are private and legal.

• Expect long delays if you are trying to receive a phone call in Accra. It sometimes takes several days to get through. The same problem exists when you are trying to call other countries in Africa.

• There are no emergency telephone numbers.

IN PUBLIC

• Remember that Ghana is a very homogeneous society. People are not encouraged to be individuals or to be creative.

• If you are angry, never express your feelings in a loud manner. Don't lose your temper, or you'll draw unwanted attention to yourself.

• Expect Ghanaians to be noisy and gregarious in a jovial and jocular way.

• Never indulge in demonstrative behavior (e.g., hand-holding, touching, kissing) with a member of the opposite sex in public.

• Don't use your left hand.

• Two gestures to remember: "Come here"—arm extended, palm out, and fingers moving to the middle of the palm and then up (it's the American way of waving "good-bye," but you don't move the whole hand up and down, just the fingers); "Good-bye"—with open palm out, wave the arm left to right.

• If you are told that an event will be on "white time," that means it will start promptly at the assigned hour.

• Bargain in stores. (Sellers will think you're stupid if you don't bargain.) However, in food markets, prices are pretty much fixed. The women owners will generally agree on a negotiated price (e.g., for several tomatoes). However, they may give you one or two extra tomatoes because you have chosen to buy from them. (Example: When one American woman wanted a huge quantity of tomatoes to make a sauce, she bought from six different women. Each one added a few tomatoes as a bonus, so she ended up with the huge amount she wanted.)

• In villages, women don't smoke.

• Always ask permission before photographing someone. Most people—especially children—like to have their pictures taken. Sometimes people will ask for money to pose.

• Don't photograph ports, airports, TV or radio stations, dams, or government buildings. If you do, you could be arrested.

• In addition, don't photograph government installations in the area around the Old Castle in Accra, where the head of state lives. Because of numerous *coup* attempts, soldiers there are suspicious.

• Avoid using video cameras. Soldiers don't like them, and if you're photographing something that you shouldn't, the camera will be confiscated.

• The only places that you'll find public bathrooms are in hotels and restaurants.

• Don't swim. Beaches are often used for toilets, fish are cleaned there, and refuse is dumped. Then the tide washes over the land, and the debris moves into the water.

DRESS

• Ghanaians appreciate foreigners wearing traditional dress. For women: A *ntama* (ntah-**mah**), a long skirt reaching to the ankles, sometimes with a slit or a pleat to facilitate walking; it's made of printed cotton, called *kaba* (**kah**-bah). The top varies according to the style of the moment. It might be buttoned in front or zipped in back or one piece to pull over the head. It may reach to the waist or to the hip and may be either loose or fitted. The headpiece is a portion of material to wrap around the head *or* to carry a baby in *or* to wrap around the waist *or* to wear as a stole around the shoulders for a more formal occasion. Sometimes women have headpieces made to wear as hats.

For men: A two-piece *batakali* (bah-tah-kah-**lee**) outfit. The shirt has very wide 3/4-length sleeves and a round neck with two or three buttons to the chest. It may reach to the hips or the knees—the one reaching the knees has two large pockets. There may be a third piece—a long, flowing robe, stretching to the ground, called an *agbada* (ahg-bah-**dah**).

• Note that Ghanaians associate clothing with wealth, so if you're wearing skimpy clothing, they will think you're very poor, even if they know better.

• For casual dress in cities, women can wear pants, skirts (not miniskirts or very tight skirts), shorts (not tight and not short), T-shirts, and thongs. Women should not wear bikini tops, except at the beach. Men can wear pants or shorts and a shirt.

• For business, men should wear a well-pressed suit and tie; there should be no "crumpled" look, or Ghanaians will think that there is someone in your house too lazy to iron. Shoes should be shined. Women should wear a dress or a skirt. (Major business will be transacted in an air-conditioned office.)

• To an evening meal in a better restaurant, women should wear good pants, skirts, or dresses; men don't have to wear jackets. To an ordinary restaurant, women can wear anything, as long as it's modest.

• For formal events—naming ceremonies, weddings, funerals—

men wear *kente* cloth, which is like a colorful king-size sheet, draped over the left shoulder with the right shoulder bare. (Very often the men shave under their arms.)

• Be aware that people in villages often receive donated clothing. Don't be surprised to see men sometimes wearing skirts. However, women never wear men's clothing. (On Sunday, people wear their traditional dress, which lasts a lifetime.)

• Don't go topless on beaches. Ghanaians will find it very offensive.

MEALS

Hours and Foods

Breakfast: Sometime between the 6:00 A.M. sunrise and 8:00 A.M. (Having breakfast very early enables people to work while it's cool.) People of modest income will have a fermented millet porridge (called *koko*) and bread with Ovaltine or *milo* (a cocoa drink). Those with higher incomes will have tea or *milo* and bread. Foreign guests will usually be offered toast.

Lunch: Noon. Typical dishes: *Kenkey,* a corn-based dough rolled inside leaves and steamed; break it apart and eat it with fried fish, cooked until it's very dry. Ghanaians eat the whole fish—head, eyes, etc. These very tiny fish are called "one man's thousand," meaning that one man could eat a thousand. Another popular lunch dish is *gari,* grated cassava grit with beans, fried plantains, fried coco-yams, fried yams, and/or rice.

Dinner: 6:00 or 7:00 P.M. In the south, where people work all day, the main meal is usually at night. Dishes are often the same as those at lunch. Another possibility is *foo-foo* (cooked cassava or plantain pounded for hours into a glutinous mass like a thick porridge) with soup or stew. Make a ball with the *foo-foo,* dip it in the sauce, and swallow it. *Don't* chew it. This can be difficult for foreigners; people will probably laugh in amused tolerance if you chew, but they realize that swallowing the *foo-foo* whole is difficult for newcomers.

Middle-class people eat rice at either lunch or dinner. It may be served with boiled yam, cocoyam, or plantain and *ampesi* (ahm-pay-see), a dish made of pounded cocoyam, cassava, or plantain mixed with water and salt and made into a thick porridge; it is served with palm nut stew (palm nuts are oily and orange) or spinach stew.

• Soft drinks (a soda similar to Coca-Cola), water (don't drink it unless it is bottled water), and palm wine (which has alcohol) are often served before a meal, but drinks aren't usually served with meals.

Table Manners

• Note that in cities the mother and children eat first and leave food for the father, who will come home later. In villages, the men eat first and have the best food. Whatever is left goes to women next and children last. A foreign woman will be served with the men.

• If you have teenagers or children with you, they will eat with the teenagers and young children in the household.

• As a guest, you will be served at a table if there is one. However, if people don't have a sufficiently large table, you may be served on a coffee table in the living room, which means that you will have to hold your plate. If the group is eating from either individual bowls, or from a communal bowl, your host and hostess will probably eat with you and serve you.

• Remember that people consider a foreign guest to be of high status, and they will want her/him to sit on a chair, even if only one is available.

• As a guest you will have a plate. Even in villages, people may send around to find you a plate. You will probably be given cutlery, but if there is none, eat with your *right* hand.

• If you offer food to a person, and he/she says, "Thank you," it means "No, thank you."

• To signal that you've finished, extend your hand, and say, "It's okay."

• Stay for a while after dinner. If you "eat and run," your hosts will think that you came only to eat.

Eating Out

• In Accra, look for Chinese, Lebanese, Indian, African, French, and Continental restaurants, as well as traditional restaurants, which serve yams and *foo-foo*.

• Street vendors sell food in leaves. Eat it *only* if: (1) your stomach doesn't get upset easily, and

(2) the meat is well cooked and hot (in temperature).

• Don't expect menus to be posted outside restaurants.

• Chop bars are three-sided structures with benches and tables; if the bar is crowded, feel free to sit with others. While Ghanaians follow the practice of bringing their own bowl, there will be an extra one for you to use.

• To attract the waiter or waitress's attention, say "Sir," "Madame," or "Excuse me."

Specialties

• Some Ghanaian specialties you may wish to try: groundnut soup, a peanut soup made of chicken, onions, carrots, peanut butter, and crushed red peppers; palm nut soup; fish soups in coastal areas; local lobster, crab, shrimp, and fish; *killiwilli,* deep-fried, ripe plantains, chopped up with ginger and hot peppers (it's made in the afternoon in markets in the south); *banku,* like *foo-foo; kenkey,* fermented corn dough, rolled in leaves and steamed.

• Ghanaian food tends to be spicy, like Mexican or Indian food.

• Peanut butter is referred to as groundnut paste.

HOTELS

• In four-star hotels, expect to find 24-hour room service, air-conditioning, same-day laundry and dry cleaning, and complimentary transportation to and from the airport.

• In small hotels, there is usually no hot water, but there are baths and clean beds.

TIPPING

• Restaurants: Hotel restaurants may include a service charge. In other restaurants, you don't *have* to tip, but you may wish to leave the equivalent of 50 cents U.S.

- Give porters at the airport the equivalent of $4.00 to $5.00 U.S.
- Don't tip taxi drivers. Negotiate the fare when you get in; there are no meters.
- Tip hotel room attendants 5% of the total bill.
- Give household help (for a one- or two-week stay) the equivalent of $1.00 to $2.00 U.S.

PRIVATE HOMES

- Since most people don't have phones, feel free to drop in, *unless* the person is of extremely high status. In middle-class or lower-class homes, to drop in unannounced is to honor a person. In these homes, someone will always be home, except on Sunday, when the entire family may be at church. Those at home will tell the person that you came to visit, thus indicating that you came to honor her/him.

- In villages, people will offer you water as soon as you arrive. Unless it's bottled water, decline, saying that you have stomach problems. An alternative is to carry bottled water with you.
- In villages, expect people to show you their photo albums and possibly to play their tape recorder when you come to visit.
- Don't use the telephone without asking first.
- Keep in mind that most people don't have household help. Family members help out. Never treat family members like servants or offer them a tip. If you need something done, such as having clothes washed, ask your hostess how you should accomplish your task.
- Remember that people in villages tend to rise early to work while it's cool.
- Don't be surprised to find that people—especially in villages—have no concept of privacy. They don't believe that sleep and space are sacred. Even if you're asleep, Ghanaians will knock repeatedly and for a long time.
- Ask for the "toilet," not the bathroom, since bathrooms are in separate rooms from the toilet.
- Most people don't have hot-water heaters. They fill a bucket and heat the water with a coil. In homes with showers, the water is

always cold. If there's a shower stall, stand in it, and scoop water over yourself. If there's no shower stall, the floor will have a drain into which the water you pour on yourself will run.

• Because of the heat, you may want to bathe more than once each day. Ghanaians usually take two baths every day.

• If you've stayed with a family, when you depart give money to the children—at most 1,500 cedis *each*. Present the money to the oldest child. In a city, say, "This is for you to buy candy." In villages, say it's for water or bread. If the children are very young, give the money to the parents. In villages, give money to adults also—about 200 cedis each. Offer the money at the very last instant—as you're dashing out the door.

Gifts: Don't bring a gift when invited to a meal—it's an insult. If you are able, reciprocate with an invitation to a meal. Write a thank-you note or call the following day. When you're leaving the country, send the family a gift— e.g., chocolates or presents for the children (exercise books, pens, etc.).

• In general, it's better to give gifts to children rather than parents.

• Don't give Muslims liquor, but other people may appreciate vodka, gin, whiskey, or cold beer.

• From abroad, bring children T-shirts or sweatshirts with a printed design (city name, sports team, university, pop singer), baseball caps, or pop music tapes. If you know the family doesn't have much money, bring clothing, such as underwear for children, shirts, or skirts.

• If you know a family well, bring sheets. Pack extra shampoo, conditioner, and nice soap, and say that you don't have room to carry it all back.

• Ghanaians also appreciate blank cassette tapes, photo albums and frames, and quality candy; women enjoy receiving perfume.

BUSINESS

Hours

Business Offices: Monday through Friday, 8:00 A.M. to noon and 2:00 to 5:30 P.M.

Government Offices: Monday through Friday, 8:00 A.M. to 12:30 P.M. and 1:30 to 5:00 P.M.

Banks: Monday through Friday, 8:00 A.M. to 2:00 P.M.

Stores: Monday through Saturday, 8:00 A.M. to 5:00 or 6:00 P.M. (no closing for lunch).

Money

• The unit of currency is the *cedi* (cee-dee), abbreviated C. Each cedi is made up of 100 *pesewas*. The cedi is the note, and the pesewa is a coin, though it doesn't exist because the currency has been devalued so much.

• Coins: 5, 10, 20, 50, and 100 cedis.

• Notes (Bills): 100, 200, 500, and 1,000 cedis.

• Remember that bringing local currency into the country is forbidden.

• Ghana has no black market.

• In most towns, you'll find a Forex bureau—quick and efficient service—for changing money.

• In Kumasi and Accra, change money at communications centers, where the rate will be better than that at a bank.

Business Practices

• Before leaving for a business trip to Ghana, contact the Commercial Attaché at Ghana's Embassy in Washington, D.C., Ottawa, or London. Another good source of business information is the Trade Ministry in Accra.

• Don't forget that who you know is very important. You won't find official sources (e.g., the Ministry of Industry) very helpful.

• Avoid making appointments during the period around Christmas (December 22 to January 3). Business continues during July and August, even though people take holidays during those months.

• Try to have someone from Ghana meet you at the airport and help you through Customs. Even with such help, it may take a few hours to complete the Customs requirements.

• If you stay at a four-star hotel, you'll have an office away from home. There will be secretarial help, photocopying and word processing facilities, translators, telex, and fax, as well as conference rooms.

• Even outside the best hotels, major cities will have private communications centers with faxes, telexes, and photocopiers.

• Be prepared to visit Ghana regularly, because businesspeople value personal relationships, and they will want to know you before entering into a major transaction.

• Be prepared to hire a translator, since not everyone speaks English. Either ask your hotel to arrange for one or get in touch with the school for translators in Ghana. If your business has a special vocabulary (e.g., engineering, electronics), specify that you would like an interpreter familiar with that terminology.

• Since there are few phones, be prepared to go in person to make or confirm appointments. Allow extra time for traffic jams. Since there are no pay phones or car phones, you have no way to let people know that you'll be late.

• Don't expect Ghanaians to be on time for meetings.

• Expect to be offered a cold soft drink when you arrive for a meeting.

• If the Ghanaian company knows Western-style business practices, women will be accepted. There are some women in the informal economy but not many in major industries.

• Don't bring a gift on your first business visit. It might be considered a bribe.

• Both business lunches and dinners are common.

• Ask your Ghanaian counterpart to choose a restaurant. If he is reluctant, ask for a recommendation at your hotel. Many people enjoy being entertained at hotel restaurants, which usually offer music and dancing. They also enjoy the cultural shows at the universities.

• Ghanaians will probably invite you to a restaurant that serves food to which a foreigner would be accustomed.

• A woman doing business alone in Ghana may find it difficult to invite a male counterpart to a restaurant, since she may be suspected of having an ulterior motive. It may be best not to send an American woman as a company's sole representative.

HOLIDAYS AND SPECIAL OCCASIONS

• Holidays observed in Ghana: New Year's Day (January 1); Independence Day (March 6); Good Friday; Easter Monday; AFRC Holiday (June 4, commemorating the day Flight Lieutenant Jerry Rawlings came to power in 1979 with his military regime); Republic Day (July 1, celebrating the day on which Ghana became a republic); Christmas (December 25 and 26).

• You might be invited to one of three special days—a naming ceremony (called an "outdooring," held one week after the birth of a child), a wedding, or a funeral. If you are served a soda or food, donate some money. People will publicly ask for money and will probably recite who has given how much. The money collected is given to the people who hosted the event. For those you know well, give the equivalent of $1.25 U.S.; if you don't know the family well, give the equivalent of 50 cents U.S.

• Note that funerals are joyous—not mournful—events, featuring drumming, dancing, and talking. People express their grief when the announcement of a death is made. The funeral itself may take place a few days or even a few months later.

TRANSPORTATION

Public Transportation

• Consider using government buses—called STC (an abbreviation for State Transport Corporation)—for long-distance travel. They are fast, large, comfortable, inexpensive, and they don't take more passengers than there are seats.

• Trains, which link Accra, Kumasi, and Takoradi, are comfortable, but they are old, slow, and use steam engines. Except for sleepers, which must be booked the day before departure, tickets are not available until the day of the trip. In first class, tickets are limited to the number of seats. In second class, there are no limits on numbers of tickets sold. A sleeper takes two people per compartment and has bunks with sheets. Expect a great demand during Christmas, Easter, and the beginning and end of school vacations. Snacks are available on the train or at stops.

• Taking a taxi from the airport will cost more than other taxi rides, but in general taxis are inexpensive. Those that travel certain routes have set fares, but if you ask for a "dropping service" (a private taxi), you have to bargain. Ask the driver what the fare is before getting in. Respond, "That's too much," and offer half. Then the bargaining starts.

• In Accra, the capital, you can share one of the taxis that goes along a designated route and will drop you off along the way, or you can take a private taxi. Most drivers think that tourists want a private taxi. If you don't, make that clear, and don't get in until someone else has entered the cab. If the driver asks if you want to "charter" a taxi, you will then be the only passenger.

• If you decide on a shared taxi, realize that the driver won't leave until it's completely full—perhaps we should say "overfull." A taxi that should hold four may be jammed with nine people, chickens, a goat, etc.

• The most expensive taxis are "fast cars"—Peugeots or Toyotas—which are driven very wildly, and very fast.

• A "lorry" is a closed van packed with people. In addition to the regular seats on each side, there will be folding chairs in the aisles.

• To hail a taxi, put your hand out with fingers pointing down.

• To tell the driver you want to get out say, "Let me down here."

Driving

• Be aware that it's less expensive to rent a car with a driver than to rent a car to drive yourself. There are other good reasons to hire a driver: (1) Street signs may not be clear (on major highways signs are good, but in cities streets may not be marked). (2) The driver might be better able to cope with the large number of reckless drivers. (3) You won't have to try to find your way through Accra's frequent traffic jams.

• Note that parking in central Accra is a problem until 5:00 P.M., when businesses close. There are no meters. Park anywhere on the street or in Accra's one parking lot.

LEGAL MATTERS, HEALTH, AND SAFETY

• When you arrive at the airport, be prepared to have a Customs official ask you for money (a bribe) to go through quickly. He'll say, "I'll be your assistant." If the savings in time is worth it to you, pay; if it isn't, don't. If you don't, you may have to go through several steps—see several supervisors and get several signatures.

• Be sure to keep the currency declaration form you're given when you arrive.

• When you arrive at the airport, many, many people will try to grab your bag in hope of getting a tip for carrying it. Don't let them take the bag.

• Don't try to take cedis out of the country. Try to convert any leftover cedis at the airport bar as you leave.

• Register any artifacts (e.g., wooden artifacts or paintings) that you plan to take out of Ghana at the National Museum in Accra. Take the form you'll be given to Customs officials when you leave the country. You may have to pay a tax.

• If police stop you for a traffic violation, don't argue. If they ask for money, pay it.

• Expect villages to be crime-free, because people fear the shame that would be brought to their family if they commit a crime.

• *Always* bring a mosquito net to avoid getting malaria. Use it even in good hotels.

• To avoid cholera, be sure that food is well cooked and *hot* in temperature.

• Be careful at beaches, because there is a very strong undertow.

• Ghana is considered to be a safe country for women. If you're in trouble, shout, and many people will come to your rescue.

KENYA

Kenya, named for Mount Kenya, the second highest mountain in Africa, has set aside large areas of land as wildlife preserves, which is why safaris to Kenya are so popular.

Nairobi, one of the key cities in East Africa, hosts the headquarters of many of the United Nations' regional services.

The climate varies according to the region of the country. The average temperature on the coast, where the humidity is high, is 80 degrees F. (27 degrees C.); in the highlands, it is 57 degrees F. (14 degrees C.).

GREETINGS

• If you know the person you're greeting well, shake hands for a very long time, but only for a short time if you don't know the person well.

• Realize that men shake hands with men and women, and women shake hands with one another. Women who are very close friends may hug in greeting and/or kiss on both cheeks.

• Expect firm handshakes.

• To show respect—e.g., to an older person or a person of senior status—grasp your right wrist with your left hand while shaking hands.

• Note that a first greeting is accompanied by a lengthy question period. You'll spend at least 15 minutes responding to and asking such questions as, "How are you doing?" "How is your family?" "Where are you coming from?"

• Women should not look men in the eye when they greet.

• In villages, people use last names.

• Be sure to use titles if you know a person has one: "Doctor" for an M.D. or a Ph.D.; Teacher; Professor.

• Call a man over 35 *mzee* (m-zee), a term of respect meaning "elder." Use this title everywhere, even in hotels and restaurants. Address a woman over 21 as *mama,* and a child as *toto.*

• With women, discuss their children and yours.

• With men and women, discuss your favorable impressions of Kenya, the climate, and your area abroad. Since politics is open in Kenya, it's an acceptable subject for conversation.

CONVERSATION

• The two official languages are English and Kiswahili (the Swahili name for the Swahili language). English, the official language of government and business, is spoken by educated Kenyans.

• Learn a few words of Swahili to earn the appreciation of Kenyans throughout the country (see "Key Phrases" at the end of this chapter).

• Never discuss sex; it's a taboo subject.

• Avoid discussing rituals—e.g., circumcision.

• Don't criticize the government or bring up the "emergency" with the Mau Mau.

• Don't ask about a person's husband or wife, but do ask about children.

• In villages, ask people about their family, their farm, their occupation, and where they're from. Ask, "How is your *shamba* (plot of land) doing?"

TELEPHONES

• Look for public phones in Nairobi and other city centers. Expect long lines at public phones. Local calls cost KSh (Kenyan Shilling) 1. Public phones take only KSh-1 and KSh-5 coins. You can purchase phone cards in post offices in Nairobi, Mombasa, and Kisumu in denominations of KSh 200, 400, and 1,000. A KSh-200 card allows you to talk to North America for about three minutes.

• To make a long-distance call, go to the post office. Wait for an operator and then wait (usually about 20 minutes) to be summoned for your call.

• Note that you can dial most international calls directly from a private home or a hotel room.

• If you need police, fire, or ambulance emergency service, dial 999. In rural areas, go through the operator, who will have the special local number.

IN PUBLIC

• If someone is speaking to you in Swahili and setting a time for an appointment or is telling you when an event is scheduled to happen, make sure to translate the time into more common usage. In Swahili time, midday and midnight are 6:00, and 7:00 A.M. and 7:00 P.M. are 1:00. Add or subtract six hours from the Swahili time (and try to figure out whether the time is for day or night). This would be a problem *only* with those speaking Swahili.

• If you're in a Masai area, expect many, many flies. You can buy brushes with handles to keep flies away.

• Keep in mind that people tend to tell you what you want to hear. If you need directions, don't say, "Is X over there?" A Kenyan will say "Yes," even if that's the wrong direction or the person doesn't know where X is. It's better to ask, "Where is X?"

• If you ask for directions in Nairobi, don't be surprised if the person walks with you to where you're going, if it isn't too far. Don't, however, follow someone down a dark alley.

• Don't pat children on the head. Pat their back, or shake hands.

• Avoid beckoning with the palm upward, because some people consider the gesture rude. Beckon with the palm down.

• Don't point with the index finger. Instead, point with the chin. Close your mouth, and push your chin forward in the direction that you want to indicate.

• If you smoke, feel free to smoke anywhere without asking permission.

• Bargain everywhere, except grocery stores, liquor stores, and department stores.

• Always ask people's permission before photographing them. Most Kenyans will want money. You *must* pay the Masai, or they may stone your vehicle. Negotiate the fee in advance. Older people may refuse to be photographed, because they believe that you are taking their soul away.

• Never photograph any building with a Kenyan flag on it.

• Note that there are public bathrooms, but many are very dirty. Try to use those in hotels, restaurants, and larger shops, where the toilets will be Western style.

• In rural areas, the toilets are of the squat type.

• The word for bathroom is *choo* (pronounced "cho").

• Bring tissues or toilet paper, because you usually won't find any in a public bathroom.

• Although some families have toilets, you may not be able to flush because of a water shortage. Sometimes water goes on for a few hours, and people fill up buckets. Use water from the bucket to flush.

• See the Introduction for information on safaris.

DRESS

• For casual attire, men and women may wear jeans, but women should not wear shorts except on safari or in a private home in a city. Safari shorts are acceptable for men.

• As a tourist, feel free to wear safari outfits—khaki shorts, pants or skirt, and a shirt.

• Note that business circles model their customs on the British. Dress is informal in the coastal region, where it's acceptable for men to wear open-necked shirts and shorts to a business meeting or to a meeting with government officials.

• If invited to dinner, men should wear jackets and ties, unless the meal is a small gathering at the home of close friends, when shirts and pants would be fine. Women should wear dresses or skirts and sandals or heels.

• Many women go bare-legged, although some wear stockings in the cooler season (April through November).

• Be aware that jacket and tie for men and dresses for women are required in hotel grill rooms, elegant restaurants in cities, and the Mount Kenya Safari Club. No such requirement exists in Mombasa.

• Only members of the diplomatic corps ever wear formal attire.

• Kenyans are impressed if Westerners wear traditional dress, providing it's worn properly. For women, the garment is the *kanga*. A single piece of material is wrapped around the body from waist to ankles; another piece is wrapped around the upper body. Foreign women may wear the *kanga* as long as they don't change the style—e.g., wear one as a halter or as a miniskirt. Men do not have a traditional costume; they wear shorts and pants.

• On the coast, in Muslim areas, women should cover the upper arms and shoulders and should wear skirts, not pants.

• Wear leather shoes, because roads and streets may be very muddy and very dusty, with rough, stony paths. Canvas shoes are easily destroyed by these conditions.

• If you're going to the highlands, take a set of heavy clothes—

warm sweater or jacket and corduroy pants—since it can get very cold at night.

• Women should wear a one-piece traditional bathing suit at the pool or beach. People are shocked by bikinis.

MEALS

Hours and Foods

Breakfast: A city breakfast, eaten between 7:30 and 9:00 A.M., consists of fresh fruit (pawpaw, pineapple, bananas) or juice, cold cereals, bacon, sausage, eggs, toast, and tea or coffee. In a village, the meal will be tea and toast, sometimes with eggs. The tea is called *chai* (chye).

Lunch: From 1:00 to 2:00 P.M., or from 12:30 to 2:00 P.M. Dishes often served: *irio,* made of dried corn, potatoes, beans, and peas, which are sometimes mashed together (a variation of this dish consists of corn, which is boiled and then fried with onions, tomatoes, and potatoes); *ugali,* white cornmeal usually served with kale which has been stewed with spices (the kale dish is called *sukuma wiki* [soo-koo-mah wee-kee], meaning "push the week")—the dish is easy to cook when you don't have much time. To eat *ugali,* make a ball of it, then make a depression with your thumb, and use the *ugali* to scoop up the *sukuma wiki.* (In villages *ugali* is eaten with the right hand, while people in cities use a knife and fork.)

Dinner: Often at 8:00 P.M., but you may be invited to an early supper at 6:30 or 7:00 P.M. In middle-class or upper-class homes, you'll be offered mixed drinks, sherry, beer, and soft drinks, accompanied by snacks of peanuts, crackers and cheese, and/or chips and dips. A dinner with a guest will usually consist of: soup or another appetizer; chicken or fish with potatoes or rice, and vegetables; bread or rolls; dessert—often a pudding. With the meal, you'll be served beer or wine. Afterwards, coffee or tea. (Note that salad is not normally served with dinner; it most often appears at a cold luncheon buffet.) The foods at dinner are similar to those at lunch.

In villages a regular meal will have just one dish. For a special visitor, there will be courses: (1) tea; (2) soda; (3) biscuits; (4) *ugali.* You will spend a great deal of time sitting and eating because people will assume that you have walked a great distance and are very hungry.

Tea: Adhering to the British tradition, Kenyans break for tea in mid-morning and about 4:00 P.M.. The afternoon tea is usually heavier, often accompanied by pastries, cakes, and sandwiches.

• Rice often appears at meals, served with potatoes and kale, cabbage, or beef. It's eaten with a spoon. Put the rice on your plate, and pour sauce over it.

• Common beverages are tea, water, milk, and soda. To avoid the water, ask for a soda, which will always be available. Passion fruit juice is widely available, but, since water is added to it, it's not safe to drink.

• As a result of British influence, beer is usually served warm.

• Realize that coffee is found mostly in restaurants. Most Kenyan coffee beans are exported.

Table Manners

• Note that at more formal dinners, the male guest of honor is seated to the right of the hostess and the female guest of honor to the right of the host. However, most often, the seating is informal and guests seat themselves.

• In cities, expect families to eat together at a table for all meals. In villages, men are served in the living room, and women and children eat in the kitchen. Guests never eat in the kitchen. They will be served in the living room, often on the only furniture the family owns. If you are the only foreign guest, you may find yourself eating *alone* in the living room (if the men are eating outside) or eating with the men. If a family has only one room, men eat outside.

• In cities, people use plates and utensils. It's not necessary to eat with the right hand only. In villages, as a foreigner, you'll be offered silverware.

• In cities, food is brought around by a servant on platters from which you help yourself.

• In villages, even though people will pressure you to keep eating, be modest in your consumption, or there won't be any food left for the children.

• Take small servings at the start, and then a second helping if you wish. While you don't *have* to finish everything on your plate, it's polite to do so.

• Eating in a village, don't say you're "full," because that means you're pregnant. Say that you've had enough to eat, or in middle- or upper-class homes, say, "Finished" to a servant.

• Plan to stay one to two hours after a meal.

Eating Out

• In Nairobi, expect to find restaurants in all price ranges, from elegant and expensive to fast-food shops and cafés. There is also a wide range in types of foods: Chinese, Indian, Korean, Middle Eastern, and *nouvelle cuisine.* In markets you'll find African restaurants, which serve barbecued goat or chicken with *ugali* (stiff maize porridge) and *sukuma wiki* (like collard greens).

• In Mombasa and along the north and south coasts, look for African, Arab, and Swahili restaurants. There are also stalls, which have goat meat kebabs, and corn or cassava roasted over charcoal stoves called *jikos.* Also available are Indian *samosas* (deep-fried turnovers with meats and vegetables) and *chapatis* (thin round bread).

• Expect restaurants to be open for lunch from about 12:30 to 2:30 P.M. and for dinner from 7:00 to 10:30 P.M.

• Check in the window to see if the menu is posted. Some restaurants follow this European practice.

• It's not customary to join strangers at a table.

• In villages and in small local restaurants in cities, expect the hostess or waiter to bring a pitcher of water to pour over your hands to rinse them. There usually isn't a towel, so you have to shake your hands dry.

• To call the waiter, say "Excuse me" or *"Bwana"* (**Bwah**-nah)—which means "Sir"—or beckon with your palm downward. *Never* call the waiter "Boy."

Specialties

• Major specialties are in the fish family: The best freshwater fish are *tilapia*, farmed trout, black bass, and Nile perch. Try jumbo prawns, small crabs, spiny lobster, and langoustines—all available but not abundant. An excellent hot and spicy dish is *prawns pili pili*, made with butter, garlic, lime juice, red chilies, coriander, and grated coconut.

• Vegetable specialties include: *muhogo ya kuchoma,* roasted cassava with chillies and lemon; *matoke,* steamed bananas; *githeri,* beans and maize; *irio,* peas, vegetables, and maize.

• Among the Kikuyu, the specialty is *githedi*—beans and corn.

HOTELS

• Keep in mind that there are four main types of accommodations: hotels, tented camps, lodges, and self-catering accommodations. Several major hotel chains are represented in Nairobi and Mombasa. If you're traveling with children, look for one of the small, clean hotels with special family rates and baby-sitting service.

• Note that prices at lodges change with the season. Some of the establishments are luxurious.

• Consider renting a beach house or apartment. Some come with a cook and a maid. Some apartment complexes have tennis courts, pools, and boat rentals.

Travel agents keep lists of these accommodations (with photos).

• Tented camps may be of the permanent type with concrete floors and adjoining bathrooms, or they may be simply a camping spot where a guide sets up a temporary camp.

• Expect a private bath in a luxury hotel. Request a private bath if you'll be staying in a moderately priced hotel.

• Keep in mind that most hotel prices don't include meals. The rate at lodges, however, includes all meals.

• Book months in advance for a hotel room in Mombasa during the Christmas and New Year's period.

• Prepare for big meals at a game lodge if you're on safari: a full English breakfast, a huge luncheon buffet with many varieties of food, and a three-course evening meal.

• Bring a hearty appetite to Kenya. Major hotels serve international foods of the highest standards. Many up-country hotels and inns serve excellent meals at reasonable prices.

• Expect many hotels to serve tea in your room at 6:00–6:30 A.M., if you wish. This is a particularly valuable service if you are on safari and have to rise early.

• Look for safe, filtered drinking water in a thermos in your hotel room, especially in a countryside hotel or lodge. Bottled mineral water, local or imported, is available in hotel shops and in supermarkets.

• Take advantage of the smorgasbord that many hotel restaurants offer on certain days.

• If you would like traditional Kenyan dishes, some large hotel restaurants will fulfill your request.

TIPPING

• Restaurants: Leave 10% unless the service is included; if so, leave 2 to 4 shillings extra.

• Most hotels, lodges, tented camps, and restaurants include a service charge of 10% in your bill.

• Porters: Give the equivalent of 50 cents U.S. per bag.

• Safari guides: Tip the equivalent of $3.00 U.S. per day.

- Safari driver: Give the equivalent of $3.00 U.S. per day.
- When drinking at a bar, leave the bartender 10% of your tab.
- Leave hotel room attendants the equivalent of about 50 to 75 cents U.S. per day.
- Tip taxi drivers the equivalent of 10 to 50 cents U.S., depending on the length of the ride.

PRIVATE HOMES

- Realize that people in Kenya are more formal than people in other African countries. They don't drop in for a visit. The usual visiting times are 10:00 A.M. and 4:00 P.M. (teatimes). Be sure to call in advance.
- Expect to be offered soda or tea whenever you visit.
- If you stay with a family, anticipate being introduced to their friends. Kenyans are very social and hospitable.

- Offer to help with household chores, but usually there are servants, even in middle-class homes.
- If you would prefer to sightsee on your own, you shouldn't have a problem. However, test out your host and hostess's feelings to see if they would be offended if they weren't included in your plans.
- Ask before taking a bath, since sometimes there are water shortages. You may find that there's a shower but no water coming from it. Take water from a bucket and pour it over yourself while standing in the shower.

Gifts: Don't bring a gift when invited to a meal in a village. People won't know how to respond to it.

- When invited to a meal in a city, bring wine, flowers, chocolates, dinner mints, or good-quality hard candy.
- From abroad, bring children toys, books, or pencils.
- People enjoy receiving the latest books, recent newspapers—e.g., *The New York Times* or the *Washington Post*—tapes, and watches. Men may like shaving lotion, Swiss army knives, and watches. Women usually appreciate lotions, bath oils, perfumes, or

scarves (long ones to drape over the shoulder, or head scarves).

BUSINESS

Hours

Businesses: Monday through Friday, 8:30 A.M. to 4:30 P.M., and Saturday, 8:30 A.M. to noon.

Banks: 9:00 A.M. to 1:00 P.M. and 2:00 to 5:00 P.M.

Government Offices: Though there are some variations, most government offices are open Monday through Friday from 8:30 A.M. to 4:30 P.M. and on Saturday from 8:30 A.M. to noon.

Stores: Monday through Saturday, 9:00 or 9:30 A.M. to 5:00 or 6:00 P.M., with a closing between noon and 2:00 P.M. A few open one or two evenings in the week; many are open Sunday until 1:00 P.M. In Mombasa, shops may open as early as 7:00 A.M., close for a long siesta break from 12:30 to 4:00 P.M., and then reopen after dark. Shops, called *dukas* (the equivalent of convenience stores—selling a little bit of a lot of things, such as cookies, soda, milk—which you'll find everywhere), may stay open well into the evening and during most of the weekend.

Money

- The unit of currency is the Kenyan shilling, abbreviated KSh. The shilling is made up of 100 cents (cts).
- Coins: 5, 10, 50 cents; 1, 5 shillings.
- Notes (Bills): 10, 20, 50, 100, 200, and 500 shillings.
- Sometimes people use the term "pound" to mean 20 shillings, and a 20-shilling note is often referred to as a "pound note."
- Expect prices to be quoted in shillings, but, for larger items, they will be quoted in pounds.
- Almost all city and major town banks have a "Bureau de Change," which may be open for more hours than the bank is.
- When you arrive in Kenya, you will receive a currency declaration form. Each time you

change money, *be sure* to have the amount entered on the form. You'll have to show the form when you leave Kenya.

• Remember that it's illegal to import or export Kenyan currency.

• If you wish, use credit cards in almost all principal hotels, lodges, restaurants, and shops.

Business Practices

• If you are a member of the Rotary Club or Lions Club in North America, you'll be able to attend meetings in Kenya and are likely to make good contacts at them. Other sources are the Kenya National Chamber of Commerce and the Nairobi Chamber of Commerce, both located in Nairobi.

• Keep in mind that personal references are very important. Networks of personal relationships are vital for doing business in Kenya.

• Avoid making appointments during the week between Christmas and New Year's and during the period around Easter. Also avoid the rainy season (April through June) because many businessmen take vacations at that time.

• From abroad, make appointments two weeks in advance.

• Bring an ample supply of business cards—in English—because it could take up to a week to have them printed in Kenya. However, there are good facilities for making photocopies. You can send faxes or telexes from the post office or from one of the private companies offering these services.

• Be punctual, but your Kenyan counterpart may not be. The more experienced a person is in international business, the more likely he is to be on time.

• If you're dealing with British or Indian firms, prepare to drink endless cups of coffee or tea.

• Don't be surprised if there is a prolonged period of personal conversation at the beginning of your first meeting. Kenyan businesspeople want to get to know you before doing business.

• Be conservative in your approach and behavior, and exercise patience when dealing with government officials.

• Note that decisions are usually made by a few people at the top of the organization.

• Be sure to obtain a written contract.

• If you're entertaining at a business dinner, include the spouse in an invitation to an elegant European-style restaurant.

their local stadium for traditional dances, performances, choirs, and presentations by schoolchildren. Around lunchtime, local political leaders speak, and a local administrator reads a speech composed by the President of Kenya (in Nairobi, he attends the celebration). The celebration is capped in the evening by a soccer game, with the winner receiving a trophy.

HOLIDAYS AND SPECIAL OCCASIONS

• Kenya observes the following holidays: New Year's Day (January 1); Good Friday; Easter Monday; Labor Day (May 1); Moi Day (October 10—commemorating the arrest of the first president of Kenya in 1952); Madaraka Day (October 20—the anniversary of the day Kenyans attained self-government); Independence Day (December 12, see below); Christmas (December 25); Boxing Day (December 26).

• The holiday *Id-al-Fitr,* celebrating the end of Ramadan, varies with the Muslim calendar.

• Independence Day (December 12) is a bigger holiday than Madaraka. Both holidays are celebrated in stadiums. At 10:00 or 11:00 A.M., people convene in

TRANSPORTATION

Public Transportation

• Note that there are two kinds of buses: public buses; and private buses called *matatus,* which are Volkswagen-type vans. Ask the cost before you get in, and bargain (if you wish) after the driver names a price. They are often very crowded and make frequent stops.

• Some buses are entered from the front, others from the rear. If possible, have correct change.

• Some large hotels maintain their own buses; they are cleaner and less crowded—but more expensive.

• On some major roads, such as Mombasa-Nairobi, there are large, fast buses.

• Try to avoid taking a bus during the rush hours (7:00 to 9:00 A.M. and 4:30 to 6:30 P.M.), because they tend to be crowded during those times.

• Remember that there are two types of taxis in Nairobi: (1) gray ones, with meters, which are regulated and subsidized by the government; (2) others, which look like regular cars—they may have a "taxi" sign on top, but they have no meters, so you must negotiate the fare with the driver before you get in.

• Hail a taxi on the street, or find one at one of the taxi stands outside hotels, cinemas, restaurants, and in the city center. You'll pay extra for additional passengers and also for baggage.

• If you aren't on a tight schedule to go a long distance, you could take a speed taxi, which is a long-distance, shared taxi. Unfortunately, speed taxis tend to break down.

• Note that Kenya Railways is fairly modern, but limited. The only routes are Nairobi–Mombasa, Nairobi–Kisumu, Nairobi–Malaba,

and Voi–Taveta in the southwest.

• Book your ticket in advance at the station or through a travel agent. In first class, you'll have a private compartment; in second class, compartments are shared; in third class, which is extremely crowded, there are just seats. Trains have no air-conditioning. Both first and second class have dining cars.

• If you're traveling alone, take your valuables with you when you go to the bathroom.

Driving

• If you plan to drive, bring an International Driver's License.

• In addition to the major international car rental firms (Hertz, Avis, Budget, National), several small companies offer rental cars and chauffeur-driven cars. Shop around for the best price; however, realize that you might be wasting time in looking for the smaller companies' offices.

• To rent a car, you must be over 23 and under 70.

• Take your passport with you to the rental agency.

• Be prepared to pay considerably more for cars with automatic transmission, since such cars are less available than those with standard transmission.

• Remember that driving is on the left, as in England.

• Be aware that the speed limit in the cities is 50 kph (30 mph), 30 kph (18 mph) in game parks and reserves, and 100 kph (60 mph) on highways.

• Don't forget that you must turn on your headlights at 6:30 P.M.

• Wear your seat belt at all times.

• In Nairobi, expect a great deal of traffic and major parking problems during the week.

• Before departing for a drive outside the cities, call the Automobile Association of Kenya (AAK). They will furnish information on road conditions. If you have a problem, look for AAK patrols on the major highways.

• Main roads are generally good, but roads often get very rough away from main areas. Dirt roads in the northern area—called *murram*—are very difficult to drive on and usually require a four-wheel-drive vehicle. In rainy periods, roads may be washed out, while in dry periods they're very dusty.

• Watch out for trucks and *matatus*. Drivers are often reckless and often have accidents.

• Note that many game parks have resident AAK mechanics.

• If you're driving in the bush, be sure to have enough gas to get you to your destination. Gas stations are few and far between outside towns. Carry a good supply of bottled water as well as one or two spare tires.

• Be prepared for a great deal of dust in the bush. Wear a scarf and avoid white clothing.

• Don't stop in the bush to talk to people, even children, especially in the Masai area. They will ask you for money, and if you refuse, they may throw rocks or hit your car with sticks.

• Lock windows and doors. Women should keep their purses on the floor under their feet. A typical trick is for one man to distract you from the driver's side (e.g., "You have a puncture"), while another person reaches in on the passenger side and grabs anything within reach. This scam takes place while you are parked or stopped at a light.

• If you hit an animal, keep driving. Even if you would like to pay, it would be too dangerous to get out of your car.

• Note that there are on-the-spot fines, and it is possible to bribe the police. Even if you haven't done anything wrong, police may stop you, hoping for a bribe.

LEGAL MATTERS, HEALTH, AND SAFETY

• Don't attempt to bring into the country any publication that could possibly be construed as pornographic (e.g., *Playboy*) or anything that might be viewed as Communist literature.

• Be aware that personal items (toiletries, soap, batteries, etc.) are more readily available in little supermarkets in Kenya than in most other African countries (except South Africa).

• Avoid swimming or bathing in lakes, rivers, or open water reservoirs because of the danger of parasitic diseases.

• Don't jog anyplace where there are wild animals.

• *Never* wander away from lodges or camps. You can be killed by wild animals, even buffalo, which appear very docile when viewed from a van.

• Deposit money and valuables in your hotel's safe.

• Be alert in Nairobi—petty crime is a problem there.

• Never leave bags or valuables in a car, even when it's locked.

• Carry a small pack in front; people sometimes slit backpacks, especially in Nairobi.

• Note that it's safer to travel with a fanny pack than with a purse.

• Don't walk alone after dark. Don't even take a shared taxi after dark. The driver may take you to an isolated area where you'll be robbed.

• Be cautious in game parks, as muggers are a problem.

• Don't hitchhike; it's too dangerous.

• Don't go into a park in Nairobi, even during the day, unless you're with a Kenyan. You would not be safe.

• Remember that if you ask directions, Kenyans may go with you to show you the way. Women alone should ask directions of women, whenever possible.

• Women alone should expect sexual harassment. Be sure to avoid isolated areas in towns and deserted paths in villages.

• Women alone should be sure to be in their hotel before dark. If you *must* go out, call a reputable taxi company; don't just look for a cab on the street. However, don't go out unless it's impossible to avoid doing so.

KEY PHRASES

English	*Swahili Pronunciation*
Hello	**jahm**-bo
Hello*	sah-**lahm**-ah
Hello†	kah-**ree**-boo
Thank you very much (reply to above greeting)	ah-**sahn**-tay **sah**-nah
Good morning	ha-**bah**-ree yah ah-soo-**boo**-hee
Good day (said from noon on)	ha-**bah**-ree mchah-nah
Good evening	ha-**bah**-ree ah-**jo**-nee
Good-bye‡	kwah-**hay**-ree
Sir	**bwah**-nah
Madam	**bee**-bee
Miss (used only along the coast)	**bin**-tee
How are you? (literally, "What news?")	hah-**bah**-ree
Good (the reply to the above question)	**mzoo**-ree
Please	tah-sah-**bah**-lee
Thank you	ah-**sahn**-tay
You're welcome	**see** neh-no

*This most widely used greeting means "Peace."
†This greeting should be used when you enter a shop.
‡Kenyans use "good-bye" instead of "good night."

Yes	ndee-oh
No	ha-pah-na
Excuse me	tah-sah-bah-lee
I don't understand	see-eh-leh-wee
I don't understand Swahili	see-eh-leh-wee kee-swah-hee-lee
Do you speak English?	jeh oo-nah-on-gay-uh kee in-gay-ray-zah?

MALI

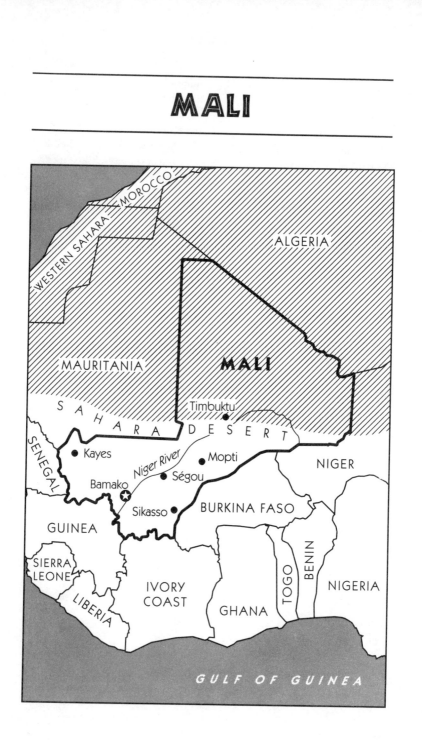

In the 5th century, when Europeans were wondering what the local Goths were up to, Mali was busy prospering because of its location on the trans-Sahara trade routes. Mali's empire reached its peak in the 14th century and then waned. The French arrived in 1866 and had conquered the country a little more than 30 years later.

One of the most sparsely settled countries in Africa (possibly because temperatures can reach 140 degrees F. [60 degrees C.] during the day in the northern desert), landlocked Mali is often referred to as a "transitional country"—between the Sahara on the north and tropical Africa in the south.

GREETINGS

• *Always* shake hands when greeting, though a man should not shake hands with a woman unless she extends her hand first. A Western woman should extend her hand to a Malian man.

• Expect a lingering handshake, a pumping of the hand, and a pumping of the forearm with the other hand. The longer these gestures last, the more respect is conveyed.

• In rural areas, after shaking hands, people may touch their heart with their right hand.

• As a sign of brotherhood, men often hold hands while walking down the street.

• Refer to people as *Monsieur, Madame,* and *Mademoiselle* with or without the last name. If you know a person's title and are speaking French, use the title—e.g., *Professeur, Docteur, Chef* (for the chief of a village).

• Even when meeting someone casually (on the street, for example), be sure to inquire about the health of that person's family.

• Hugs are not common, even among close friends.

CONVERSATION

• Note that the official language of Mali is French, but the language most often spoken is Bambara. Very few people speak English, and few speak French outside the capital, Bamako.

• Expect Malians to be very warm, hospitable, sincere, accepting, and polite. They enjoy long, personal conversations. Though you may be asked personal questions, don't respond by asking Malians personal questions.

• Don't make flattering remarks about someone's wife, since Mali is basically a Muslim country, and don't ask how many children someone has.

• People enjoy joking and teasing, but don't join in unless you know someone very well. People often make jokes that are critical of others (e.g., about the way they talk, the color of their skin, etc.); the object of the teasing joins the laughter. If people joke about your physical characteristics, take the matter lightly—never seriously.

• Don't talk about your house abroad, your salary, or anything else that touches on your social standing.

• A good subject of conversation is your positive impressions of Mali.

• Don't touch people while talking to them unless you know them well, and don't point to people.

• Never look people in the eye. Even children will not look you in the eye. The lack of eye contact does not signal disrespect.

TELEPHONES

• There is only one telephone booth in Bamako, but public phones are available in hotels and post offices (called P.T.T.). Rates for international calls are incredibly high.

- Don't try to find an English-speaking operator. Operators speak only French.
- Answer the phone: *Allô.*
- There are no special numbers for emergencies.

IN PUBLIC

- Malians are generally quite reserved but very kind. They tend not to give vent to frustrations, so it's shameful to yell at another person.
- Don't kiss or hold hands in public.
- Don't bargain in stores, but it's okay to do so in markets. You won't find vendors in markets aggressive.
- In smaller towns, vendors sometimes approach vehicles. If you don't want their wares, just say "no" politely. They won't bother you, since they aren't pushy.

- It's very rare to see a woman smoking, but many Malian men smoke.
- Don't expect people to dote on their children as they do in other countries.
- Always ask permission before photographing someone. Most Malians enjoy having their photos taken; however, they may expect a copy. If you don't have an instant camera, ask for names and addresses, and *be sure* to follow up by sending a photo back.
- In some Muslim countries in Africa, women believe that it's against the Koran to be photographed. However, in Mali, Muslim women seem to enjoy having their pictures taken.
- Don't make a big deal out of photographing bare-breasted women. (In practice, they usually cover themselves when a foreign man or woman is present.)
- Never photograph anyone in uniform.
- Where they exist, public restrooms are usually awful. European toilets are rare—toilets are usually the squat type—and toilet paper is almost never available. The only places where you'll find decent public restrooms are in first-class hotels in Bamako.
- In hotels and good restaurants, there will be separate fa-

cilities for men and women, labeled *Hommes* (Men) and *Dames* (Women).

DRESS

• Remember that Malians always try to look their best, even in villages. Don't wear shabby attire—torn jeans, etc.

• It's acceptable for women to wear pants (loose-fitting ones), but it's easier to develop a good rapport with Malian women if you wear long dresses, similar to those local women wear. Women should be sure to dress modestly, because Mali is a traditional society.

• Neither sex should wear shorts. Women who wear shorts are considered "loose," while men who wear shorts are considered silly, unless they are playing a sport.

• Casual dress is fine for all but the most formal occasions—e.g., meeting the President of Mali.

MEALS

Hours and Food

Breakfast: Between 7:00 and 7:30 A.M. The usual food is millet, in the form of a porridge, with coffee, if the family can afford it. Affluent people have rice with a sauce, most likely a peanut butter sauce called *tiga diga na* (**tig**-ah **dig**-ah **nah**).

Lunch: About 2:30 P.M. Working people usually leave work at 2:30 P.M. and go home for a big meal. Typical dishes: rice and sauce (often a tomato, onion, and vegetable sauce); a salad of cucumbers, onions, and tomatoes with oil and vinegar; and sometimes fruit such as mangoes or papayas (in season) for dessert.

• If guests are eating with a family, the sauce will always include meat. The wealthy *always* have meat—goat, beef, or chicken—at every meal. Sauces always accompany meat.

Dinner: Sometime between 6:00 and 8:00 P.M. Foods will be the same as those at lunch.

• Eat tomatoes and other vegetables *only* if they are peeled.

• The beverages usually served with meals are tea, water, or soda.

• Malians often chew kola nuts. They give the chewer a caffeine-like jolt.

• Be aware that mealtimes are always arranged around the Muslim prayer times.

Table Manners

• Note that children often eat separately from their parents, and men and women often eat in different rooms.

• Malians usually eat—with the right hand *only*—from a common bowl. If you're sharing a meal with Malians, consider sitting on your left hand so that you won't accidentally use it to reach for food. The practice of eating from a single bowl is not so unsanitary as one might think, because each person keeps to her/his section of the bowl. Backing away from the bowl signals that you're finished.

• In all but the most traditional village homes, expect to be given a fork, a spoon, and a plate.

• If invited to a meal in a village, bring your own bottled water. Tell your hosts that your stomach is not accustomed to the local water. Try to get comfortable doing and saying this, because the consequences of drinking the local water can be extremely unpleasant.

• Don't anticipate the offer of a drink with alcohol. Mali is a Muslim country.

• People tend to have beverages after the meal. They eat quickly and then sit and chat afterward.

• You may be invited to a tea ceremony. A teapot is filled with water, stuffed with tea leaves, and then put on a brazier. When the water is boiling, it's poured back and forth between the full kettle and an empty kettle. After more heating, the tea is poured into tiny glasses. Sometimes each person has a glass, and sometimes there is just one glass. There will be huge amounts of sugar. Take as long as you want to drink the tea, even if there's only one glass for the group. There are three "rounds" to the tea ceremony. The first serving is strong. After the tea is poured, the teapot is refilled with water. Thus, the tea becomes weaker with each serving. Usually, the company at a tea ceremony includes just men or men and women. A "women-only" tea ceremony is rare.

Eating Out

• In Bamako, you'll find French, Lebanese, Chinese, and Vietnamese restaurants. You will also find cheap food stalls that sell *brochettes* (shish kebab), fish, *ragoût* (stew), rice, fried plantain, potatoes, sweet potatoes, couscous, and beans. The food should be safe to eat, because the meats and vegetables are cooked for a very long time. However, before buying food, make sure that it's hot in temperature.

• To call the waiter, say "chef," *not "garçon."* In this context, "chef" refers to a chief, not a chef who cooks. Another term used to summon the waiter is *teri kay,* which means "friend."

Specialties

• Popular staples are millet mash, sorghum mash, and corn mash.

• Other special foods: grilled goat or mutton; grilled fish; rice (regarded as a special dish) with a peanut-based sauce; and *riz au gras* (rice cooked with oil and vegetables).

HOTELS

• Note that hotels tend to be either elegant or "dumps" with very little in between.

• Unless you're in the very best hotels, don't expect to be provided with soap or toilet paper.

• Realize that the *few* medium-range hotels may not have hot water but they usually will have air-conditioning; however, the air conditioners are probably old and may provide air that is either too cold or not cold enough. Since these hotels normally don't have screens, mosquitoes will be a problem. Though these hotels will furnish towels, they don't provide soap or toilet paper.

• Most Westerners would not be comfortable in the lowest-class hotels (even though they may offer air-conditioning). Most are very dirty and don't offer hot water, soap, or toilet paper.

• Electricity in hotels sometimes goes off—but not very
often.

PRIVATE HOMES

TIPPING

• Tipping isn't necessary at a
restaurant *(service compris)*.

• Give porters and bellhops the
equivalent of $1.00 to $2.00 U.S.,
depending on how many bags
you've asked them to carry.

• Tip washroom attendants the
equivalent of 10 to 30 cents U.S.

• If you've had a car and driver
for a week, tip him the equivalent
of $2.00 to $4.00 U.S. per day,
depending on the level of service
provided. If the driver is not eating lunch with you, give him the
equivalent of $1.00 to $2.00 U.S.
for lunch per day.

• When visiting someone, don't
knock on the door. Stand outside
the door, and clap twice.

• If you go into a home while
the family is eating, they will insist
that you join them. Hospitality is
very important to Malians.

• Follow your host's lead about
whether to follow the custom of
removing your shoes before entering a room.

• In the morning in a Muslim
home, people wash first, pray
next, and then have breakfast.

Gifts: If invited to a meal,
bring tea or sugar (Chinese green
tea is the favorite). If you're staying with a family, give cloth: bring
about five yards of a synthetic fabric, which Malians prefer because
it's easy to care for and lasts a long
time.

• For children, bring jars of
soap bubbles, balloons, or balls;

young people will enjoy a T-shirt with a city name on it.

• An unusual but welcome gift: kola nuts, which are available in any market. Malians can afford them, but to offer them as a gift signals respect. To eat one, bite off a tiny bit, and chew it. The stimulant effect lasts about two hours. Men and women chew kola nuts, but children do not. Kola nuts are an especially welcome gift in remote villages, where they are difficult to obtain and are relatively expensive.

BUSINESS

Hours

Businesses, Government Offices, and Banks: Monday through Friday, 7:00 A.M. to 3:00 P.M., usually with a lunch break between 1:00 and 2:00 P.M.

Stores: Monday through Friday, 8:00 A.M. to noon and 3:00 to 6:00 P.M., and Saturday, 8:00 A.M. to noon.

Money

• The unit of currency is the CFA franc. (CFA stands for *Communauté Financielle Africaine*— African Financial Community.)

• Coins: CFA 5, 10, 25, 50, and 100.

• Notes (Bills): CFA 500, 1000, 5000, and 10,000.

• Try not to change traveler's checks often, since a flat-fee commission is charged each time. Change your checks at banks; their commission is lower than that at the hotels that will change traveler's checks (mostly the large hotels in Bamako).

• Expect to use your credit cards only in first-class hotels, expensive restaurants, and for car rentals.

• Mali has no black market.

• You may bring in to Mali or take out as much of the local currency as you wish.

Business Practices

• To establish contacts with businesses in Mali, use one or more of the following sources: (1) the Mali Embassy in Washington,

D.C., Ottawa, or London; (2) the Mali Desk Officer at the Department of Commerce; (3) the Commercial Section of the American Embassy, Canadian Embassy, or British Embassy in Bamako; (4) the Chamber of Commerce—*Centre Malien du Commerce Extérieur;* (5) for banking—*Banque du Développement de Mali;* (6) for people interested in investments in transportation—*La Coopérative des Routiers Transportifs.*

• Remember that habits derived from the French persist—for example, seeing an important person is a major event. If you make your contacts through your embassy, and they call on your behalf, your mission will be regarded as prestigious.

• Avoid scheduling business trips at the following times: (1) the rainy season—June through September (a slow business period); (2) the last week in December, when people vacation; (3) during Ramadan and other Muslim holidays (dates vary). Allow plenty of time in Mali to accomplish your business goals.

• For the best chance of success, send a senior person from your company for the initial meetings. This demonstrates that your company is serious, and the senior person will receive preferential treatment. Be especially sure to

send a senior person when a high government official will be involved in the negotiations.

• Never dress casually for a business meeting. Men should wear suits and ties; women should wear dresses or suits.

• Remember that English is not widely spoken. French is the main language of business. If you are not fluent in French, find an interpreter either through your hotel or through your country's embassy. If you are in a business that utilizes special vocabulary, be sure to give that information to the person seeking an interpreter for you.

• If possible, make appointments in the morning.

• Be flexible, because people's schedules often change.

• Be on time, but don't be surprised if Malians are late. If a person has been assigned to pick you up at your hotel, be prepared for him to be late.

• Be sure to bring business cards. They need not be translated into French. Give one to everyone you meet.

• Don't call people by their first names right away. Wait until they use yours.

• If the meeting begins according to Malian tradition, an exchange of greetings will be followed by the Malians offering you a drink. Then they will say "Welcome," which means "What can we do for you?" You should thank the Malians for taking the time to meet with you. You can then explain the reason for the meeting.

• Be respectful but never condescending.

• Be sure that any written materials are translated into French. If you plan to use graphics, which can be helpful, be sure that your Malian counterparts have projectors for slides or overheads. If not, you'll have to bring your own, with appropriate adapters for the electric current (220 volts AC).

• Note that you can send faxes and telexes from hotels or from the post office. Though the hotel charges are exorbitant, they may be worth it, since otherwise you'll have to stand in line at the post office.

• Try to bring any photocopied materials you will need with you, since there are few places to make copies in Mali.

• If you're passing out materials—or giving anything to another person—be sure to give (and accept) with your right hand *only*.

• As a first step, try to establish a good and trusting relationship with your prospective business partners. Make sure to put them at ease as to your business ethics, through discussions and social engagements. Show an interest in the local culture, especially Malian history. Discuss your positive impressions of the country and what you've learned about the culture, particularly Mali's glorious past. In a non-boastful way, make people aware of your accomplishments in other business dealings. Your host will probably inquire about your trip to Mali and your family.

• Show respect for older people, even if they have nothing to do with your negotiations.

• Expect business to be conducted slowly, with bureaucracy likely to be a problem. How quickly business is accomplished depends on the Malians' educational background and the country in which they have trained (i.e., someone trained at Harvard Business School will tend to move forward more quickly).

• If your dealings are with a minister whose schedule is full, he may meet with you for only a short time.

• Remember that bargaining is a major part of the Malian tradition. Pad your cost estimates a bit so that you'll have room for give-and-take. Don't be too eager to discuss the bottom line. Focus on selling your idea first; after that you can raise the subject of price.

• In a private-sector company, the senior executive will make the decision. However, if you're dealing with the government, more than one ministry may be involved. Any contract over a certain amount has to go through a central purchasing office, which makes sure that the contract conforms to government regulations—that no bribes have been paid, and that prices are fair.

• Women own many retail stores and food markets. You will also find them in the government and on the police force. However, the more formal business sector is dominated by men. Since Malian men have a chivalrous attitude, women may be able to get better results than men. If your company's Vice President for Marketing is a woman, by all means send her to Mali.

Business Entertaining: Don't suggest or expect an invitation to a business breakfast.

• People may not invite you to their home because they live in crowded conditions and are embarrassed; they fear that they won't be able to entertain you in the style to which they believe you are accustomed.

• If you suggest a meal in a restaurant, you have indicated that you will be paying. Chinese restaurants are the most popular for business entertaining.

• A spouse may decline your invitation to a business dinner because of language problems.

Gifts: Good business gifts: a picture book of your city or region; a calculator; a desk calendar; a good pen.

• Don't bring a gift for your first meeting, but if a relationship develops with a Malian, feel free to offer a parting gift.

HOLIDAYS AND SPECIAL OCCASIONS

• The following are holidays observed in Mali: Armed Forces Day

(January 20); Labor Day (May 1); African Liberation Day (May 25); National Independence Day (September 22); Christmas (December 25).

• Two holidays in the Muslim calendar fluctuate: one is Ramadan; the other is Tabaski (69 days after the end of Ramadan), which celebrates both the end of the pilgrimage to Mecca and Abraham's preparation to sacrifice Isaac (when a ram appeared and was slaughtered instead of Isaac). In the morning, men pray in the mosque. Afterwards, they slaughter a sheep, and spend the day grilling the meat. Malians wear their very best clothes on Tabaski.

TRANSPORTATION

Public Transportation

• Note that privately owned Peugeot station wagons are the main means of public transportation in Bamako. The drivers stuff them with people and usually will not depart until the car is full.

• You'll find an inter-city bus and shared taxi system. If you take a taxi, ensure your comfort by paying for two seats—and be sure you get the extra space.

• If you take a taxi from the airport to a major hotel, the price will be fixed. To other places, negotiate the fare beforehand.

• In Bamako, you'll see small pickup trucks with benches (called *bah-shay*) that locals use. They're not for the fainthearted, but a ride on one could be fun if you're feeling adventurous.

• Don't expect local train service. Two trains run the Bamako–Dakar route, one Senegalese and the other Malian. If you have a choice, take the Senegalese train.

Driving

• Car rentals are available, as are cars with drivers. To drive yourself, you can use your own driver's license or an International Driver's License. However, it is *much* better to hire a local driver, who will speak French. Involvement in even a minor fender-bender can be dangerous.

• Driving in Bamako is a nightmare. Horn-blowing is constant, and you'll encounter huge potholes in those roads that are paved.

• Another road hazard is animals—goats, sheep, chickens. If you hit one, stop and apologize to the owner. Whether or not you have to pay depends on whether the animal's owner thinks that you were driving recklessly.

• Police may stop you in hope of a bribe. The police are paid so poorly that they can't live on their salaries. Be friendly and respectful, and engage them in conversation. If you say that you don't have any money, the request may be dropped.

• Should you be stopped for drunk driving, you may be able to talk your way out of the problem, if the police regard you as having sufficiently high status. Otherwise, you may have to pay a fine on the spot.

LEGAL MATTERS, HEALTH, AND SAFETY

• Consider *every* body of water (whether you're thinking of drinking it or swimming in it) a potential source of bilharzia—a parasitic disease that causes fatigue, extreme exhaustion, and even death.

• Never eat salads or uncooked fruits or vegetables.

• Mali is a very safe country, but it's best not to go out at night. Street crime isn't the problem that it is in more affluent African countries. Though violent crimes against foreigners are rare, pickpockets are everywhere.

• Children may approach you and ask for money, but they will not harass you.

• Women traveling alone may be bothered (verbally) by Malian men, but they won't be physically molested. To minimize the possible problem, wear loose-fitting clothing with skirts below the knee.

KEY PHRASES

The following phrases are in Bambara.

English	*Bambara Pronunciation*
Good morning	ih nee **so-goma***
Good afternoon	ih nee **woo**-lah*
Good evening	ih nee sue
Good-bye	**kan** ben
Thank you	ih nee **chay**†
You're welcome	No equivalent
Yes	ohw
No	**ah** yee
Excuse me	ha **kay** toe
I don't understand	n ma **fa** mu
Does anyone speak English?	**mo**-go bey anglikan fo?

Here are a few French phrases.

English	*French Pronunciation*
Good day	bawn-**zhoor**
Good evening	bawn-**swahr**
Please	seel-voo-**pleh**
Thank you	mehr-**see**
You're welcome	de ree-en
Yes	wee

*For the phrases beginning "*ih nee*," a man should respond "*mba*," and a woman should respond "*nsay*."
†This expression is also used as a general greeting.

No	nawn
Mr., Sir	meh-**syeu**
Mrs., Madame	mah-**dahm**
Miss	mahd-mwah-**zehl**
Excuse me	ex-kyou-zay **mwah**
Good-bye	o reh-**vwahr**
I don't understand	zhe ne kawn-prahn **pah**
I don't speak French	zhe ne pahrl pah frawn-**seh**
Do you speak English?	pahr-lay voo ahn-**gleh?**

NAMIBIA

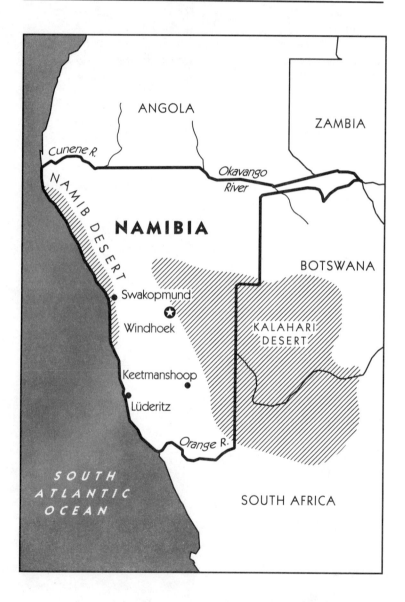

ANGOLA

ZAMBIA

Cunene R.

Okavango
River

N
A
M
I
B
DESERT

NAMIBIA

BOTSWANA

Swakopmund

★ Windhoek

KALAHARI
DESERT

Keetmanshoop

Lüderitz

Orange R.

SOUTH
ATLANTIC
OCEAN

SOUTH AFRICA

Because of its location on the southwest coast of Africa, Namibia became popular with European trading countries—the Portuguese, the Dutch, the British, and the Germans. After they departed, South Africa took over the country and refused to give it up. The ensuing struggle for independence cost Namibia dearly in many aspects of normal life—business, education, and agriculture.

As the country recoups, it is actively courting tourists with enticing information about the game parks, and businesspeople with opportunities for investment.

GREETINGS

• Expect everyone to shake hands in greeting—men and men, men and women, women and women, and even children and elders.

• When shaking hands with blacks, shake hands, and, while still holding hands, link middle fingers, and shake again. Don't use this informal handshake when you are first introduced.

• Note that not everyone has a first name, especially if they haven't been baptized. Use a person's Christian name or African name with nothing preceding it. Example: "Franz Mpepo" is some-one with a Christian name and a Namibian name. Sometimes people would call the person "Franz"; other times "Mpepo." Originally, people did not have Christian names but acquired them as a result of Western imperialism.

• Titles in common use are: Minister (for a government minister), Reverend (for a pastor or a bishop), Doctor, and Professor. Use first names with friends and titles and last names with people you don't know well.

CONVERSATION

• Although English is the official language, Afrikaans, German, and

11 other, native languages are spoken.

• Avoid bringing up the war Namibia fought to gain its independence from South Africa, and don't ask to which political party a Namibian belongs. Although political discussions are not taboo (Namibia is rather open in this area), you need to tread cautiously on any political ground.

• If you don't know whether a woman has a child or not, don't raise the subject, since women without children are considered by many to be an embarrassment.

• Good topics for initial conversations with men: family, children, and their work.

includes a helpful business guide in the Yellow Pages.

• Telephones in Windhoek (the capital) are automated, and from them overseas calls can be dialed directly. You may use a credit card, or you may call collect.

• The public telephones found in post offices have meters on the phones to let you know when the money you've deposited is running out. If you wish to continue the call, be sure to put more coins in before the time elapses; otherwise, you'll be cut off.

• Keep in mind that telephone operators speak English.

TELEPHONES

• Expect very efficient telephone service in Namibia; however, sometimes the connection may not be clear.

• The single telephone book, which covers the entire country,

IN PUBLIC

• Always defer to elders. Never contradict an opinion one has voiced.

• Expect Namibians to be subdued—very different in manner from West Africans. Never behave in a loud, boisterous manner.

• When visiting a village where you don't know anyone, try to meet the chief and request his permission before wandering around.

• Always ask permission before using water from community bore holes.

• Be aware that until the late teenage years, young people are very affectionate with members of the *same* sex. Young girls walk with arms around one another and play with one another's hair. Boys are similarly affectionate with one another.

• Prepare for prices in shops to be fixed. Bargaining is acceptable only when you are purchasing expensive curios and artwork and when you are dealing with artists selling their own crafts. Prices on those items are usually so low that you may wish to pay the asking price.

• Always ask permission before photographing people. Some—especially in rural areas—expect money or a gift such as a T-shirt. Such requests will be most common in the northwest, where the Himbas live, and in the eastern part of Namibia, where Bushmen live. However, these areas aren't those that usually attract tourists.

• Don't photograph any government properties.

• Look for clean Western-style public toilets in malls in Windhoek. In other areas, public toilets are very primitive.

DRESS

• Always dress neatly in clean clothes in both cities and villages. If you wear sloppy or torn clothes, Namibians won't respect you.

• For casual dress, women can wear slacks, and men can wear Bermuda shorts (never short shorts). Women should never wear bikini tops.

• Remember that people in Windhoek dress more formally than people in other areas, though farmers in outlying areas are also conservative. In Windhoek, neither sex should wear shorts or safari outfits.

• Be aware that you won't be allowed into elegant restaurants in shorts or sandals.

• When visiting mission stations, former tribal areas in the north, or rural areas, women should wear skirts below the knee or loose cotton pants.

• If you visit during the winter (May through September), be aware that mornings and nights are *cold,* with the temperature sometimes dropping to freezing. At noon the sun will be hot. Be sure to pack a warm sweater and/or jacket, and plan to dress in layers.

MEALS

Hours and Foods

Breakfast: In a modern home in the city, families will have eggs and bacon or sausages (called *boervors*) between 7:00 and 8:00 A.M. Some breakfasts also offer beans or potatoes, and sometimes steak. The beverage will be coffee or tea.

In the countryside, breakfast is between 7:00 and 8:00 A.M. People will have bread and butter, if they have access to a store. Most likely, they will have *mealie pap,* a porridge-like dish made from maize. The breakfast beverage is made from sorghum, sugar, and water.

Lunch: In cities, between noon and 2:00 P.M. The meal will be a large one—a rice dish or vegetables with millet and meat in homes of blacks; whites will eat meat or fish and potatoes and a vegetable. In modern homes in the city, lunch and dinner show the European influence, with a great emphasis on beef.

In rural areas, lunch, eaten between noon and 2:00 P.M., will consist of sorghum, which is thicker than porridge, and spinach. If people can afford it, there will be goat. To eat the dish, dip the sorghum into the meat and sauce.

Dinner: In villages, this main meal of the day is eaten between 9:00 and 10:00 P.M. Options for dinner include millet porridge with a stew of beef or chicken, or possibly rice with stew.

City dwellers eat at the same time. They may have meat (beef is extremely popular; other options are lamb or chicken), potatoes, a vegetable (which varies according to the season, because vegetables must be imported from South Africa), salad, and a dessert of cake, pastry, or fruit.

During the autumn harvest season, Namibians in rural areas eat boiled groundnuts (peanuts) or roasted corn after the meal. During the day, rural people eat boiled beans.

• Note that Namibians eat a great deal of beef and also bratwurst (a German sausage).

Beverages: In modern households in cities, drinks are usually offered before dinner.

• In villages, where drinks are served before and/or after the meal, the choice will be either soda or a fermented drink made from boiled water, millet meal, and sorghum meal, called *oshikundu*. *Oshikundu* is offered to guests, whatever the time of day that they visit.

• Be aware that alcohol isn't sold in supermarkets. You must buy it at a bottle store—*drankwinkel*—open all day, except at lunchtime and on Sundays.

Table Manners

• Be punctual when invited to a meal. (This rule of thumb applies throughout southern Africa.)

• Expect family members to eat together, sitting on a mat on the floor. They will eat from a common dish, though sometimes each person has an individual plate. Eat just enough to sustain yourself, not a tremendous amount.

• When eating from a communal bowl, use only your right hand.

• Realize that whites in cities emulate European table manners—knife in the right hand and fork in the left. They also follow the European rule of keeping the wrists on the table, never in the lap.

Eating Out

• In Windhoek, you'll find a variety of restaurants—from German, Italian, and Chinese to pizza and burgers.

• Many restaurants specialize in German dishes, while others focus on game—kudu, springbok, oryx, warthog, and ostrich.

• For tasty German pastries, cakes, and apple strudel, stop at one of the many German *Konditorei*.

• You'll find good cafés in Windhoek and Luderitz and small coffee shops in other towns. The cafés serve alcohol, mainly beer and wine.

• For take-out places, look near liquor stores; the usual menu offers sandwiches *(brotchen)*, oryx pie and chips, or fish and chips.

• Fish lovers should order fish in restaurants on the coast, where the fish is fresh.

• Some restaurants offer Afrikaaner desserts, such as *koeksisters* (a sweet dumpling) or *melktart* (milk tart).

• For the best coffee, seek out one of the establishments run by Germans.

• In large towns, take advantage of a money-saving trick favored by many travelers: a picnic. You can buy spit-roasted chickens, all types of sausages and salamis, and various kinds of breads.

• Note that menus are posted outside restaurants, in the European fashion.

• In casual restaurants, feel free to seat yourself. In better restaurants, wait to be seated.

• On Sunday, you must order a meal in order to have an alcoholic beverage.

HOTELS

• When considering accommodations, keep in mind that hotels, caravan parks, campsites, guest farms, and safari companies are all graded with the following star system:

1-Star: Private baths or showers for 25% of the rooms; 16-hour floor service for light snacks. Few have air-conditioning, but all are clean and comfortable.

2-Star: Private bathrooms or showers for 50% of the rooms; 16-hour floor service; 14-hour reception service.

3-Star: Private baths; wall-to-wall carpeting; rooms and lounges; à la carte menu; room service; guest transport. (There are only four such hotels in the whole country.)

4-Star: An air-conditioned palace with salon, valet service, and a full range of services for the business traveler. (There is just one in Namibia—the Kalahari Sands in Windhoek.)

• Most hotels have a TV in a common room, and some have a radio in each room.

• Realize that guest farms are more expensive than hotels and must be booked well in advance, since they generally have just six rooms. These working farms provide interesting insights into rural life. The farms are often luxurious and provide very personalized service. Some are reserved for hunters during the hunting season, while at other times they're open to tourists interested in game viewing.

• The 10% hotel tax is customarily included in the quoted room price.

• If you'll be visiting Namibia off-season, ask if the hotel offers special rates—most do.

• Every hotel has a bar, but some bars are quite simple and don't serve fancy cocktails. Many hotels also have beer gardens.

• All hotels serve three meals a day, typically including a great deal of meat. For example, breakfast might be eggs with curried kidneys or bacon or *boervors* (a heavy farmer's sausage) or steak.

• Large hotels offer a breakfast buffet, which is included in the room price.

• Expect to find laundry service in even the smallest hotels. Resorts and campsites have washing machines.

• Note that all water from hotel faucets is purified and thus safe to drink.

TIPPING

• Leave 10% of the check for waiters.

• Give taxi drivers 10% of the fare.

• Tip porters the equivalent of 75 cents U.S. per bag.

• It's not customary to tip hotel room attendants. If you wish to tip, the amount is entirely at your discretion.

• Tipping the household help in a private home is a good idea, but be sure to ask your host or hostess what to tip in order not to give such a huge amount that your hosts may be embarrassed.

• Tipping is illegal in the resorts

and game parks operated by Nature Conservation, but this rule is generally ignored. If you wish to tip, give the driver and/or guide the equivalent of $3.00 U.S. per day for game runs.

PRIVATE HOMES

• Among the European community, people call ahead before visiting. Africans tend to drop in. In rural areas, visitors don't call ahead, because most people don't have telephones.

• If you're staying with a family in Windhoek, there is normally constant hot water. People tend to bathe daily except during the winter, when they conserve water a bit. If there's an obvious drought, and you can tell that people are concerned about water levels, don't bathe every day.

• In rural areas, it's not unusual for several women to sleep in the same bed, curled up with one another.

Gifts: If invited to a meal by city dwellers, bring a bottle of wine. If invited to a meal in a village, women should bring sorghum, millet, or rice, but men needn't bring anything.

• Good gifts from abroad: baseball caps, T-shirts, barrettes, earrings, pens, audio cassettes of American gospel or spiritual music, and clothing (if you know sizes).

BUSINESS

Hours

Businesses: Monday through Friday, 8:00 A.M. to 4:30 P.M., and Saturday, 8:00 A.M. to 1:00 P.M.

Government Offices: Monday through Friday, 8:00 A.M. to 5:00 P.M.; closed Saturday.

Banks: Monday through Friday, 9:00 A.M. to 3:30 P.M., and Saturday, 8:30 to 11:00 A.M.

Stores: Monday through Friday, 8:00 A.M. to 1:00 P.M. and 2:00 to 5:00 P.M., and Saturday, 8:00 A.M. to 1:00 P.M. (Many stores in Windhoek are open without break all day long and sometimes stay open until 6:00 P.M.)

Money

• The currency is the Namibian dollar, made up of 100 cents.

• Coins: 5, 10, 20, and 50 cents, 1 and 2 dollars.

• Notes (Bills): 5, 10, 20, and 100 dollars.

• There is no limit to the amount of foreign currency or traveler's checks that can be brought into Namibia.

• Most hotels, restaurants, and shops accept credit cards, but many shops and hotels will *not* accept foreign traveler's checks, so be sure to carry enough cash.

• Namibia has an 11% sales tax. Purchases sent from shops to overseas addresses are exempt from it.

Business Practices

• A good source for business contacts is in the Namibia National Chamber of Commerce in Windhoek.

• Make appointments four to six weeks in advance. If you're dealing with government officials, keep your schedule loose, since they are out of the country frequently. However, you can have a much tighter schedule when dealing with private businesses. Since the weather is nice and you won't lose time during midday, you can schedule as many as eight appointments in a single day.

• Avoid suggesting business meetings during December and January. Namibians take long holidays during these months.

• Make appointments for any time during the day.

• Expect Namibian businesspeople to be open about networking and arranging introductions to people whom they think you would like to meet.

• Most businesses don't have answering machines, making it very difficult to leave messages outside of office hours.

• Note that telex facilities are available to all businesses in urban areas. As fax machines are becoming more popular, bureaus have opened in major towns for sending and receiving faxes. Inquire at a bank or a post office for the location of one nearby. If you are staying at a medium-size or large hotel, you will probably be able to send and receive faxes there.

• Anticipate the offer of tea or coffee at the opening of a business meeting.

• Be prepared for socializing before business. Namibians will ask about your family, how your trip has been, if the weather has been agreeable to you, etc. Such exchanges don't take a long time, but they may be frustrating to someone coming to Namibia on a first business trip. However, you must observe these "niceties" to ensure the goodwill of your business counterparts.

• Note that Namibian business society in Windhoek is very sophisticated, and people will appreciate your bringing graphics and visuals to illustrate your presentation.

• Foreign businesswomen should experience no problems in Namibia.

• Namibian businesspeople do not expect gifts. However, if you develop a good working relationship with someone and sense that he/she would like a particular item (computer software, for example), feel free to bring it.

• Realize that a great deal of socializing accompanies business dealings—lunches and dinners in both restaurants and homes.

• If you decide to entertain in Windhoek, you will find German, French, and Chinese restaurants but very few fancy restaurants.

• Include spouses in invitations to dinner in a restaurant.

HOLIDAYS AND SPECIAL OCCASIONS

• Namibia celebrates the following holidays: New Year's Day (January 1); Independence Day (March 21); Good Friday; Easter Monday; Ascension Day (40 days after Easter); Workers' Day (May 1); Cassinga Day (May 4); Africa Day (May 25); Heroes' Day (August 26); Human Rights Day (December 10); Christmas (December 25); Family Day (December 26).

• On Independence Day (March 21), different ethnic groups perform dances, the President and various ministers give speeches, and people feast on goat and beef.

• Cassinga Day (May 4) commemorates those who lived in exile and were killed in a refugee camp.

TRANSPORTATION

Public Transportation

• For short distances, your best bets are taxis or a rental car.

• To get a taxi, either phone for one or go to a taxi stand. You won't be able to hail a taxi on the street. All taxis have meters.

• In villages, drivers of private vehicles seat people in the back of a truck. They don't operate on a set schedule. Pay whatever the driver asks. There is no bargaining.

• Although there is train service between all major towns, journeys are arduous because trains stop frequently and are slow.

• All trains have first, second, and third class, except the train from Windhoek to Cape Town/Johannesburg, which has only first and second class.

• Trains are never fully booked because most people don't want to endure the slow trips.

• Long-distance bus service is limited. However, it is one of the better ways to get around the country. Twice weekly a bus runs between Windhoek and Cape Town/Johannesburg. Windhoek to Cape Town takes 18 hours, and Windhoek to Johannesburg takes 20 hours. Although the time is oppressively long, the buses are comfortable. They have snacks, hot meals, videos, music (with two channels), cushions, and blankets.

• Another service runs between Windhoek and Walvis Bay and Windhoek and Tsumeb every day except Saturday.

• Reservations can be made at travel agencies.

• Namibia Air, the national airline, has several scheduled flights per week to and from major centers in Namibia. It is probably the best choice for long distances.

Driving

• Realize that car rentals are expensive, and you can hire cars only during the week during business hours unless you've made arrangements in advance.

• If you arrange to pick up a rental car at the airport or train station when you arrive, be sure to confirm the plans several times.

• As a tourist, you will need an International Driver's License.

• If you plan to drive a great deal, rent a medium-sized car with air-conditioning. Any additional cost will be well worth it.

• Note that driving is on the left, as in Britain.

• Be aware that seat belt use is compulsory.

• Parking is easy in Windhoek. There are meters and parking lots, where fees tend to be modest.

• Don't worry about reading road signs. They are the standard international signs.

• Keep in mind that the usual speed limit on open roads is 120 kilometers per hour (about 70 miles per hour). Drive more slowly on gravel roads. The speed limit in built-up areas is 60 kph (about 35 mph), unless a sign is posted indicating another speed.

• Main roads throughout Namibia are paved. Even the secondary roads made of gravel are well maintained. On the coast, there are "salt" roads, which are gypsum soaked with brine to form a hard, smooth surface.

• Remember that in the rainy season (December–April), gravel roads can be damaged, making it impossible to visit some parts of the country.

• Tips for driving on gravel roads, which are usually very dusty: (1) Wrap your camera or other important items in several layers of plastic. (2) Don't drive over 80 kph (about 48 mph). (3) Reduce your speed substantially if another vehicle is coming in the opposite direction. (4) Drive in ruts made by other vehicles. (5) Don't drive at night. (6) Watch out for animals—e.g., kudu, baboons, and warthogs.

• Be sure to pay attention to signs warning of wild animals, especially kudu, because they run across the road. If you are driving at night (which you should try to avoid), go slowly, since animals are dazzled and sometimes hypnotized by headlights.

• Realize that police do spot checks around holiday time, because too many people drink and drive. If you are caught, you pay a fine later—not on the spot.

LEGAL MATTERS, HEALTH, AND SAFETY

• When dealing with Customs officials, police, chiefs, or government officials, be polite and deferential, and never show anger. These people are generally open and friendly (compared to their counterparts in other African countries). If you become aggressive, the transaction will take much longer.

• There is no black market in Namibia.

• In Namibian game parks, there are strict rules. You must book accommodations before arriving. You must sign in and sign out. You must be in a car, closed truck, or minibus.

• It's safe to drink tap water, but don't drink from bores in rural areas. If you have to drink this water, boil it for ten minutes, or use special purifying tablets.

• When traveling in the desert, always carry a large supply of bottled water with you.

• Don't carry large amounts of money in Windhoek because of an increase in muggings there.

• It's safe for women alone to walk around towns—except in unlit areas at night.

• A woman alone may be viewed with suspicion in rural areas, because people will wonder why she's not at home with her family. Carry photos of your family with you.

NIGERIA

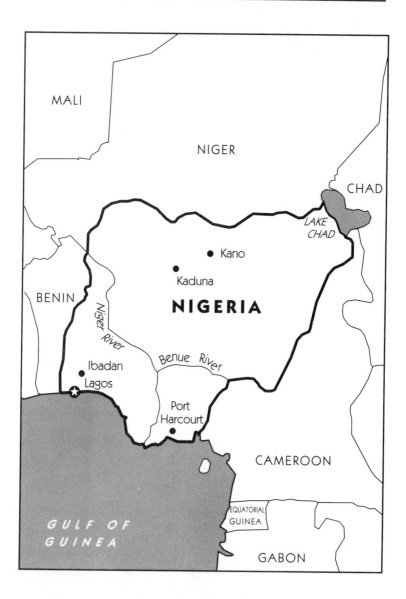

Nigeria is both the most populous country in Africa and site of Lagos, the largest city in sub-Saharan Africa. The country includes 250 ethnic groups, most with their own languages (and some of those languages have separate dialects!). The largest groups are the Hausa-Fulani in the north, the Ibo in the east, and the Yoruba in the west. (The Hausa-Fulani are predominantly strict Muslims, so women must cover their hair, and men and women don't congregate together.)

Climate is determined by distance from the ocean and elevation. For example, rainfall along the coast (where cloud cover is nearly constant) is about 130 inches per year (3.10 meters), while it is a mere 26 inches (0.7 meters) per year along the northern border. Temperatures are warm, with maximums of 95 to 105 degrees F. (37 degrees C. to 41 degrees C.).

GREETINGS

• When introduced, people shake hands with one another: men and men, men and women, and women and women. However, good friends don't usually shake hands. Women may hug other women friends.

• If someone has a title—Doctor, Barrister, Chief (a title accorded to someone who has achieved a degree of eminence)—be sure to use it.

• If you don't know people well, refer to them as "Sir" or "Madame" (accented on the second syllable).

• If you attend a group function with a Nigerian, he/she will introduce you to others. If you go alone, people will usually come to you and introduce themselves.

• Note that the Yoruba, a major ethnic group, will applaud at the arrival of an important guest.

• Don't use first names until you know people well. Be especially careful to stick to last names with older persons or persons of high status. Eventually, they may invite you to use their first name.

• Children always address older people by their last name.

• Always ask, "How's your family?" even if you don't know any family members.

CONVERSATION

• Nigerians speak three major languages, which represent the three major ethnic groups: Yoruba, mainly in the south; Ibo, in the east; Hausa, in the north. From high school on, all education is in British English. In cities, most people speak English. In villages (where people often speak pidgin English), you'll always find at least one person to translate for you.

• Never ask anyone a question without first greeting her/him. If you do, people will be offended. Even when asking directions, be sure to greet the person first. Example: Don't say, "Could you tell me where the post office is?" Say, "Good morning. Excuse me. Could you tell me where the post office is?"

• Avoid discussing religion, politics, and colonialism.

• If you meet a woman who is pregnant, don't mention it unless she does. Nigerians think that discussing the pregnancy or birth could bring on bad luck.

• Don't ask *men* how many children they have. One reason is that it will bring bad luck if one counts one's children. There's also the question of how many partners—with various trails of children—a man may have. However, it's okay to ask a woman if she has children.

• Expect people to be curious about the U.S. and jobs there.

• Ask questions about Nigeria and its rich culture.

• Keep in mind that people are quite direct (which may sometimes make them appear arrogant); they will tell you exactly how they feel without hiding anything.

• Don't back away if people get close to talk to you. People of the same sex tend to stand very close when speaking.

TELEPHONES

• Nigeria has been digitalizing the phone exchanges in some areas, so service is improving slowly. However, few people have home phones, and there is no Directory Assistance and no way to learn the charge for a call.

• Look for public phones in airports, hotels, and at certain government offices. Deposit a 50-kobo coin to make a connection.

• In some homes, where people have paid extra for the service, you can make international calls.

• NITEL is the central telephone exchange, with three major satellite uplinks in Lagos and two other towns. In a small town it is difficult to impossible to get a phone line, and you may have to travel a long distance to a large town to be able to get a line. Small towns have a phone booth at the central exchange, but the booth may be locked at unusual times. If

you ask why, the response may be, "Madame went to market."

• Pay for your call in advance. Book for a specific number of minutes. It may be worthwhile to book for more minutes than you think you'll need, since you'll be cut off at the end of your allotted time. Occasionally the operator will wave at you, signaling that your time is almost up. Try saying, "Oh, please, just one more minute." Sometimes you'll get the extra minute.

• All good-size cities have business centers that offer private telephone services, as well as fax and typing services. You make your phone call and pay when you have finished. The business centers are usually much more efficient than NITEL (the government telephone monopoly).

• People who have illegal phones may charge a lower rate.

• The number for all emergencies is 999.

IN PUBLIC

• Remember that Nigerians are quite conscious of age differences. In approaching a superior or a much older person, people usually bow. Never harshly disagree with a superior or a much older person. Be subtle if you have a difference with one.

• Always defer to mothers with children. Motherhood is revered in Nigeria. For example, be sure to give up your seat on public transportation to a mother.

• If you see a Yoruba wink at a child, it's a signal for the child to leave the room.

• Don't give or accept anything with the left hand.

• Avoid pointing the sole of the foot or showing it to another person.

• Don't use the "thumbs up" gesture. It's considered obscene. Since this is the hitchhiking sign in the U.S., don't use it when hitchhiking, or drivers will think that you are insulting them.

• Another gesture to be avoided as obscene: the hand held forward at the shoulder with fingers spread, palm facing another person. It means, "You could have any of five fathers."

• Don't photograph anyone without asking first.

• Be very careful not to get drunk. Nigerians will look down upon you if you do.

• Feel free to bargain in markets but not in stores.

• Look for public bathrooms in hotels and restaurants. Those in cities are modern and are labeled in English. There are no washroom attendants. Be sure to bring tissues or toilet paper with you.

DRESS

• Nigerians spend a great deal of their income on clothes and are always extremely well dressed. The national dress for men (with some variations) is a tight-fitting tunic and pants with a huge embroidered robe (called *baban riga*—**bah**-bahn **ree**-gah) over it. Standard dress for women is called a wrapper—a six-yard piece of material, cut into three two-yard pieces. One piece is wrapped around the waist like a skirt; one is made into a top, and one is used as a head scarf or shawl or to tie children onto the back. There's no accepted way to tie the scarf around the head, so wearers can be creative.

• Nigerians appreciate visitors wearing the national dress.

• Note that there is no "dress code" in Nigeria, except for formal business occasions. For example, at an academic conference, some men might wear shirts and trousers, some might wear suits, and some might wear traditional dress.

• For casual wear, it's okay for foreign women to wear slacks on the street in cities. Nigerian women wear pants only at home or at the beach. Women should not wear pants in villages. Men can wear shorts in the city, but women shouldn't. In general, it's best for women to stick to dresses and skirts.

• When visiting senior company executives or government officials, men should wear a suit and tie. For business, women should wear a dress.

• Be aware that some restaurants and clubs in Lagos require men to wear jackets and ties.

• If an invitation states that the event is formal, men should wear suits and women should wear long cotton dresses.

• *Never* go nude on a beach. It's acceptable to wear a bikini. Wear your bathing suit under clothing, since people don't change on the beach.

MEALS

Hours and Foods

Breakfast: Between 7:00 and 9:00 A.M. In cities, breakfast is British style: cereal, eggs, and bread, with coffee, tea, or hot chocolate. In villages, people eat a cereal called *akamu* (made from farina), bread (made from cassava), or deep-fried bean cake. With that they will have herb tea and fruits. People in villages don't drink juices.

Lunch: Between 1:00 and 2:00 P.M. For a family, this main meal may be a vegetable stew eaten with *garri* (**gah**-ree)—made of pounded roots of cassava, which are then fried or broiled. If guests are coming, rice may be the center of the meal; it will probably be served with tomato and pepper stew and beef, fish, or chicken.

Dinner: Usually 7:00 or 8:00 P.M. Most popular are rice and fish or fried plantain with a stew of chicken or beef.

• There is no custom of a coffee break because of the large meal at lunch.

• At lunch and dinner, expect dishes from three basic food groups: carbohydrates, vegetables, and meat or fish.

• In the north, the Hausa diet is based on ground grains—e.g., corn, millet, and sorghum. The grains are boiled into a porridge, *tuwo,* which is eaten with a sauce of okra, onions, tomatoes, and a little meat. (Large portions of meat are reserved for special occasions.) Peanut oil is often used in cooking. The basis for drinks is honey, sugar cane, and kola nuts.

• In the south, where the Yoruba live, *garri* is a typical dish

often followed by fruit—e.g., bananas, papayas, pineapple. Company are served cakes.

• Many men don't drink at home, but they often drink outside—including Muslims and born-again Christians. At home, people usually drink soft drinks or water.

• In homes in the city you will be offered drinks. Your host will tell you what's available—whiskey, brandy, soda water, etc.

Table Manners

• There are no rules about promptness for social occasions. Be fairly prompt for a small dinner party in a home. However, for a larger dinner (probably a buffet), arrive about 30 minutes late. (If someone refers to "Nigerian time," it means that one should be 30 minutes to an hour late.)

• Among the middle and upper class in cities, expect the meal to be served British style. Everyone will sit at a table, the food will be served from platters placed on the table, and people will use knives and forks. In villages, people usually eat (always with the right hand) on a mat on the floor.

• If your host or hostess doesn't seat you, sit where you want.

- In a polygamous family, the father will eat separately from wives and children.
- If you're invited to dinner in a home, your hosts will usually prepare Western-style food for you.
- Be sure to avoid fresh fruits and vegetables unless they can be peeled, and then be sure they are.
- Don't be surprised to see more food than you think will be consumed. People always cook extra food in case someone drops in.
- Remember to use only the right hand when eating.
- Expect meat to be served well done. Nigerians never eat rare meat.
- Beverages accompanying a meal are usually beer, water, or soda. Don't drink water unless you know it's bottled water.
- Always praise the food, and try to finish everything on your plate.
- If you're eating Western style, indicate that you've finished eating by placing the fork and knife side by side horizontally across the plate.
- If you smoke, ask permission to do so at the end of the meal. Never smoke between courses.
- If dinner starts at 7:00 or 7:30 P.M., plan to leave around 10:00 P.M.

- Advice if you are host: Don't serve pork, and always offer soft drinks if you are serving alcoholic beverages.

Eating Out

- In Lagos, several restaurants offer both Lebanese and French food. You'll also find Indian restaurants.
- If you have a taste for Chinese food, seek out a Chinese restaurant in a hotel. They are the best.
- For a little adventure, try one of the *bukas*, informal restaurants that serve traditional Nigerian food; they are often very good. You will always find rice and *garri* (pounded cassava) available, and may find goat meat or special fish dishes. Forks and spoons are the eating utensils. Be sure to order bottled water or soft drinks.

Bukas are dirty, and it may take you a while to summon the courage to go in. With their high turnover, food isn't lying around for a long time. Since the trade is largely local, they don't want customers to become ill—or they're out of business. Ironically, the food may be safer to eat than hotel food. At hotels, meat is refrigerated; power may go off for long periods, and the food will spoil.

Food is eaten so quickly at *bukas* that it doesn't stay around for days.

• Be sure to make a reservation to dine at one of the better restaurants.

• Expect to find menus posted in restaurant windows. If one is not, feel free to ask to see a menu before deciding if you wish to patronize the restaurant.

• To summon the waiter, raise your hand or make eye contact.

• Remember that when you go out to eat with a group, only one person—the one who issued the invitation—pays.

Specialties

• Among the Yoruba, you'll find these special dishes: *eba,* which is made from grilled, ground cassava mixed with hot water, and which you dip into stew (you aren't supposed to chew it); *futu,* made from the peelings of yams; *amala,* made from grated yam peelings, pounded and mixed with water, and which is used to scoop up sauce.

HOTELS

• Note that the Nigerian Tourist Board is in the process of classifying hotels, motels, and guest houses throughout the country. In large cities, you'll find hotels in all ranges: expensive, medium range, and inexpensive.

• Expect many appliances— e.g., TV, phone, air conditioner, refrigerator—in even the medium-priced and inexpensive hotels, as well as in university guest houses. *However,* one or more may not work, since maintenance money has not been available. In general, the air conditioners work.

• Realize that even the best hotels have problems with water supply and electricity. The hot-water heater may be outside your room door so that the hotel staff can monitor it to ensure that it isn't on all day.

• When registering at a first-class hotel, prepare to pay a deposit equal to twice the price of the room.

• Most large hotels have facilities for sending telexes and telegrams.

TIPPING

• At restaurants, tip 10%.

• Give porters or doormen the equivalent of 75 cents to $1.00 U.S.

• Don't tip taxi drivers; the flat rate includes the tip.

PRIVATE HOMES

• Note that it is not customary to call in advance of a visit. People just drop in. In large cities, most people have telephones, but outside cities many people don't. If you don't know someone well, call in advance of a visit.

• Expect to be offered soda and, perhaps, beer. In the poorest homes you may be offered water. (Remember not to accept tap water; plead stomach problems.) You may be asked if you want a "hot drink"—meaning an alcoholic drink, usually brandy or schnapps.

• To reciprocate for having a meal in someone's home, invite them out to a meal.

• Feel free to take a daily bath. Nigerians bathe daily and expect guests to do so as well. There may not be a hot-water heater, since few Nigerians can afford one.

• Offer to pay for any phone calls you make from a home. Your host will probably refuse.

• Note that most wealthy families have household help. If they do—and you've stayed with the family for several days or more— tip the servants approximately 20 naira each at the end of each week.

• If you're staying with a family that does not have servants, offer to help with the daily chores.

• If you wish to offer compliments on a home, keep them general. Don't say, "That's a beautiful vase," because your host may feel obliged to give the vase to you. Say, "You've decorated this room beautifully."

Gifts: If you bring a gift when invited to a meal, your Nigerian hosts may feel that you're doubting their hospitality. It's acceptable to bring a bottle of wine (except in Muslim areas). Better yet, reciprocate with an invitation to a meal, or bring toys as gifts for the children in the family.

• To give someone a kola nut is a sign of friendship. Kola fruit grows on trees and looks like a large grapefruit. When the fruit is ripe, the green skin peels away, and the silver-and-pink nuts are revealed. Nigerians chew the nuts to quench their thirst; the fruit also contains a mild alcoholic stimulant.

• Nigerian women love to receive jewelry, perfume, and fabric (e.g., brocade, jacquard, or ankara—African printed cotton cloth available in the U.S. and Switzerland). Six yards of fabric are required to make a native dress.

• If you know a family, ask before you leave your country what they would like you to bring. They may need something very utilitarian—e.g., dishwashing liquid—because of shortages in Nigeria.

• Other good gifts from abroad: T-shirts or chocolates. If you know someone has a VCR that can use European or American videos (that is, they have a multiple system), bring videos of American films.

BUSINESS

Hours

Government Offices: Monday through Friday, 8:00 A.M. to 3:30 P.M.

Businesses: Monday through Friday, 8:00 A.M. to 5:00 P.M.

Banks: Monday through Friday, 9:00 A.M. to 1:00 P.M. Many stay open on Thursday until 3:30 P.M.

Shops: Monday through Saturday, 8:00 or 9:00 A.M. to 5:00 P.M.

Money

• The unit of currency is the *naira* (abbreviated "N"), made up of 100 *kobo*.

• Coins: 1, 5, 10, 25, and 50 kobo.

• Notes (Bills): 1, 5, 10, and 20 naira.

• Be aware that bringing local currency into Nigeria is prohibited.

• Major hotels and large restaurants accept credit cards.

• Exchange your money at a bank. On the black market you may be given counterfeit currency.

Business Practices

• Good sources of business contacts in Nigeria are the Nigerian Desk, U.S. Department of Commerce, Washington, D.C., and the Nigerian Association of Chamber of Commerce in Lagos.

• Don't try to do business without a trip to Nigeria. Nigerians like to conduct business face-to-face to determine how serious you are—in other words, to get a feel for you as a person.

• Consider sending older people to do the negotiating because Nigerians are respectful of age and connect wisdom with experience.

• Make an appointment at least one month in advance, and confirm it before you leave for Nigeria.

• Avoid suggesting appointments during the week before and the week after Christmas or during Ramadan (Nigeria is half Christian and half Muslim). Also avoid travel to Nigeria during the rainy season in the summer, since getting around would be difficult.

• Allow at least two weeks in the country so that you can first establish rapport (since personal relationships are very important) and then negotiate (which may take a while).

• Be sure that one of your first stops is at the U.S. Embassy or Canadian Embassy or British Embassy in Lagos to see the Commercial Attaché.

• While faxes, copying machines, and computers do exist, they are scarce. Thus it's a good idea to include in your delegation someone with the authority to make decisions, since communicating with a home office for approval may take a great deal of time.

• If you have initiated the arrangements with Nigerian firms, you will have to make your own reservations and get to your appointments by yourself. However, if the Nigerians have sought you out and are anxious to do business with you, they will pave the way. Your accommodations will be arranged, a Nigerian will meet you at the airport, you will be given a car and driver for the duration of your stay, and you will be picked up at your hotel.

• Many companies have guest houses with maid service for visiting businesspeople.

• Remember that the first business meeting will probably take place in an office rather than at a lunch. Once you have established a good relationship, you'll be taken to lunch.

• Expect a meeting to start about 10:00 A.M. (never before breakfast).

• Be prompt. People who are Westernized will be punctual, while others tend to be late. However, foreigners are expected to be on time.

• Bring business cards. They should contain the title by which you want to be addressed: "Dr. Jones," "Ms. Smith," etc. Cards in English are fine.

• Most Nigerians in the business world speak English.

• To begin business conversation, try to learn if your Nigerian counterpart has trained abroad. Discuss that for a while, or sports, (soccer, wrestling, polo, or cricket) or other trips (to conferences, for example) your counterpart may have made. Nigerians also enjoy talking about the cultural heritage of their particular ethnic group and about Nigeria's industrial achievements. Don't go directly to the point; try to establish rapport first.

• Don't expect refreshments to be served at a business meeting, though you may be offered coffee or tea. Be sure to accept or your counterpart may be offended. If the meeting will last all day, a catered meal or snacks will be delivered to the office.

• Try to negotiate only with top people. If you deal with the lower echelons, the people will simply waste your time. If you have a contact in Nigeria, that person will pave the way for you to deal with the decision makers.

• Be formal and respectful. Your Nigerian counterpart will most likely be extroverted and talkative. Be aware that in general Nigerians are tough negotiators and may be openly critical.

• Don't worry about government red tape. The people you're negotiating with will take care of government regulations.

• Except in Muslim communities, women are fairly well integrated in business life. With many women doctors, lawyers, and businesswomen, women have a higher status in Nigeria than in other African countries. Westernized Nigerian women are used to exercising authority over men in a business setting (although men are the patriarchs in a family setting). Many women get local, state, and federal government contracts and employ men. Women are heads of government departments and hold important posts in the Civil Service. Thus, a North American company should not hesitate to send a woman to do business. (A Danish company recently sent a group of women engineers, who had no difficulty being received in the Nigerian business community.)

Gifts: Bring a gift on your first visit. Good choices would be a small sculpture, an interesting glass object (such as a paperweight)—something that will adorn the office stylishly. If you are meeting with a top-level manager, bring something special. Bring a more modest gift to a middle-level manager.

• Don't bring anything suitable for the home. Such a gift is inappropriate unless you know the person very well.

Entertaining: If you are hosting Nigerians at a meal, choose a Nigerian restaurant *only* if you are

familiar with the customs and the food. You will impress Nigerians by your knowledge of their culture; on the other hand, you risk giving offense unintentionally. For example, if you weren't aware that Nigerian sauces are *very* hot, tried one, and said, "Oh, this sauce is so hot! Give me water quickly," you would make a very bad impression.

On the other hand, if a Nigerian invited you to such a restaurant and the same thing happened, it wouldn't be a problem.

• For entertaining, stick to European, Chinese, or Indian restaurants. Be sure to do the ordering in advance.

• You may be invited to a meal in a home. If so, be sure to accept.

• In restaurants, when there are foreign guests, cutlery will usually be provided, even though most people eat with the right hand.

• Don't include spouses in lunch invitations, but do invite them to dinners.

the most important holiday for West African Muslims. Celebrations center on eating and visiting friends, after many hours at the mosque.

• During the Christmas–New Year's period, enjoy the carnivals, masquerades, and dancing in town squares during the evening.

HOLIDAYS AND SPECIAL OCCASIONS

• The following holidays are observed according to the Christian calendar: New Year's Day (January 1); Good Friday; Easter Monday; National Day (October 1); Christmas (December 25 and 26).

• The following Muslim holidays are observed: Ramadan; Tabaski (commemorating the moment when Abraham prepared to sacrifice his son to God; it coincides with the end of the Hajj, the pilgrimage to Mecca); Mohammed's birthday (celebrated on the eleventh day of the third Muslim month).

• On Tabaski people slaughter sheep and give one-third to the poor, one-third to friends, and one-third to the family. Tabaski is

TRANSPORTATION

Public Transportation

• Within cities, take shared taxis; though they are called "shared taxis," you can rent an entire one for yourself. Look for them in motor parks.

• Trains are inexpensive but slow. For long distances, first class offers a sleeping berth, a toilet, and fans. Third class is crowded and uncomfortable. On certain days, you can take an air-conditioned train. Dining cars are available on most trains.

• For long distances, top-of-the-line buses, which usually travel at night, are comfortable and sometimes air-conditioned. You will probably have to get your ticket the previous morning at a certain time. Don't be surprised if there is an armed guard on board the bus.

• Another method of travel between cities is by station wagon, which will be more comfortable and will be faster than going by bus. You can hire the whole car for yourself if you don't want to wait until it's full. You'll find these wagons in special parking areas.

• Two types of Peugeot 504 are used as bush taxis. Some take just five passengers, and others take eight. The journey can be dangerous because the drivers go so fast.

• If you want to hitchhike, it won't be difficult. Make it clear at the outset that you can't pay, because a driver may try to charge you. Don't use the American hitchhiker's sign (it's an obscene gesture); instead, stick your arm straight out, and raise your hand up and down at the wrist.

• If you want to fly to cities within Nigeria (there are often three to four flights per day between major cities), plan to arrive at the airport several hours in advance, if the airline won't allow you to reserve ahead of time. Expediters will offer to help you buy a ticket, but don't agree to this, since many are crooks.

Driving

• If you plan to rent a car, get an International Driver's License.

• Major car rental agencies are represented in Nigeria. However, it's best to rent a car with driver, because then you won't have to deal with the police yourself. You will also not have to worry about parking in cities. It is often difficult to park; in addition to which there are fines, and your car may be towed.

• If you choose to drive, don't be surprised if you're stopped by the traffic police—called "Yellow Fever," because of their yellow shirts. It's most common for white people to be stopped, even when there has been no traffic violation. The police may get in your car and tell you to drive to the police station. Knowing how much to offer as a bribe is difficult, even for Nigerians. Offer a five-naira note. Try not to negotiate. If the person claims it's not enough, avoid increasing the bribe or the price will go higher and higher. Be firm, and remain calm. Don't be intimidated. Since the "request" for a bribe is illegal, the police will want to get the process over as quickly as possible.

• You'll encounter roadblocks everywhere, and police there accept bribes. This is a form of begging, since police are not paid a living wage, and they need money.

• In general, it is safer to hire a car with a driver because if you are white and are involved in an accident, local people may overreact and become very aggressive. In this case you should drive directly to the nearest police station to report the accident.

• Expect to find roads in a bad and hazardous state. Another problem will be Nigerian drivers, who are generally reckless.

• Nigeria has no seat belt law.

LEGAL MATTERS, HEALTH, AND SAFETY

• To take art objects out of the country, obtain permission from the Nigerian Museum in Lagos, especially if the objects are made of bronze.

• Always carry your passport with you, since you may be stopped frequently by the police. However, be sure to keep your passport well hidden.

• Nigeria has no law regarding drinking age.

• If you like to gamble, you'll find casinos in most towns.

• Should you become ill, look for a doctor through connections you have with an embassy, a major foreign company, or sophisticated Nigerian friends.

• Don't go out at night. In Lagos, don't even walk around in the vicinity of your hotel. Major crimes—including armed robberies by gangs—are a serious problem in cities. Taxi drivers at the airport are involved in many of the thefts from foreigners. Avoid arriving at the airport at night, if possible. Ask dispatchers for a taxi driver whom they know, and write down the license plate number of the taxi, while the driver is watching. Don't get in a taxi if there is a person already in it.

• As a result of the high number of crimes, parties that were formerly held at night are now held on a Saturday or Sunday afternoon. The crime problem surfaces even in areas where major diplomats live.

• Crime is not so prevalent outside Lagos and Ibadan.

SENEGAL

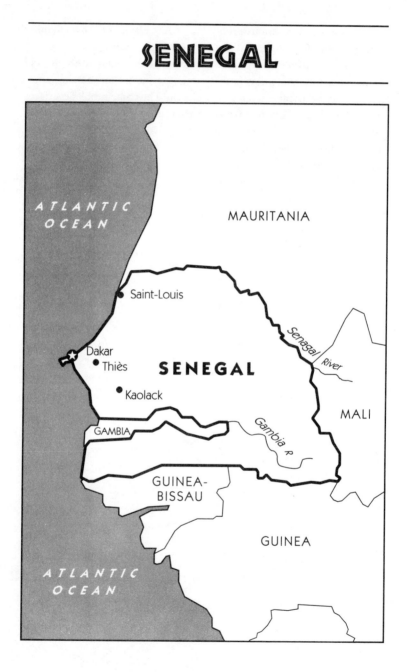

This westernmost country in Africa was a magnet for visiting European traders, and then it was bounced between England and France until in 1815 it finally became a colony of France, the country from which it achieved independence in 1960.

Like many African countries, Senegal has a wet/dry climate—a dry season from October to June and a wet season from July to October.

Since 95% of the population is Muslim, travelers should pay special attention to the section on Islam in the Introduction.

Lovers of Antoine de Saint-Exupéry's *The Little Prince* will want to visit central Senegal, where the baobab tree (which figures so prominently in Saint-Exupéry's tale) is one of the dominant forms of vegetation.

GREETINGS

• Don't forget that long greetings are very important. Keep shaking hands while asking about the health of each family member. In turn, a Senegalese will ask you if you have peace, how your health, family, and work are, and how the local weather is agreeing with you. *Always* respond that everything is fine.

• In a group, shake hands with each person both when arriving and when departing.

• In cities, greetings will be short and will be given in English or French.

• Don't shake hands with a Senegalese woman unless she extends her hand first.

• Senegalese men usually shake hands with Western women.

• A handshake is customary between men and men. It should be *very* gentle.

• Always look people in the eye when you shake hands. Otherwise they will feel slighted.

• Good friends kiss one another three times—first left cheek, then right cheek, then left cheek again. The custom is left over from the French.

• *Always* shake hands with your right hand.

• Titles to use: Docteur (M.D. or Ph.D.); Professeur; *Adja* (ah-djah) for women or *Alhadji* (ahl-hah-djee) for men: these titles, which show respect for older people or people who have made the pilgrimage to Mecca, can be used alone or with the last name.

• Never walk by an adult in a house without greeting her/him.

CONVERSATION

• Note that the official, government-sanctioned language is French, but most people speak Wolof. English is spoken in tourist areas.

• After the lengthy greeting, tell people why you are in Senegal. Then they will question you. Expect inquiries about your personal life. Women will be quizzed regarding their marital status.

• Keep in mind that women who don't work outside the home are more reserved and are not free about discussing their personal lives. However, professional women enjoy telling how they achieved success, because it was a hard road.

• You may encounter traveling storytellers *(griots),* called *toutes couleurs.* Local people will appreciate it if you ask about the *griots'* stories.

• Avoid commenting on the friction between Senegal and Mauritania, a years-old tension. Drought and political oppression brought many Mauritanians to Senegal. As merchants and traders they often prospered, and the Senegalese believed that the Mauritanians were exploiting them. After a bloody battle, the Mauritanians were expelled, but they are now allowed back in Senegal. Nevertheless, the issue is still a touchy one.

• Keep in mind that most Senegalese are interested in talking about economics but not about politics.

TELEPHONES

• In large cities there are pay phones. For three minutes, deposit 50 CFA and dial. If you don't add more money before the time is up, you will be cut off. If no one answers, your money will be returned. You can also go to the PTT (central telephone office). There you place your call and pay when you've finished.

• If you make a call from a private phone (in a home), be sure to pay the family for the call when you have finished.

• From Dakar, phone calls are easy to make and go through quickly. In rural areas, a phone call may take an hour or more to place.

• When answering the phone, say "*Allô.*"

IN PUBLIC

• Remember that Senegalese never rush. Prepare to wait in stores and at public gatherings.

• Always use your right hand when giving or accepting anything—food, a book, a tool, etc.

• Don't be surprised to find streets blocked off five times a day so that religious Muslims can pray.

• Don't kiss or be demonstrative with a member of the opposite sex in public. (One American woman was taken to the police station for kissing her boyfriend on the street.)

• Expect Wolof to be aggressive and assertive. They also express emotions easily.

• If you smoke, always offer others in the group a cigarette.

• Don't bargain in supermarkets in cities, but bargain everywhere else.

• In markets, expect vendors to be persistent and pushy. If you don't want their wares, say "No" firmly and move on. If you want to purchase something, try making an offer, then walking away (after the merchant has tried to get a higher price), letting the vendor chase you and offer a better price.

• Taking photos is not a problem. The Senegalese government is the most lenient of any in West Africa in this respect. Nonetheless, don't photograph military installations.

• Don't be surprised if people ask to be paid for being photographed.

• If you want to photograph individuals at a public gathering, be sure to ask permission first.

• You'll find public bathrooms only in restaurants and hotels. They will be labeled *"Hommes"* for men and *"Femmes"* for women. Most of the toilets will be of the squat type. While you will not find toilet paper, there will be water for washing.

DRESS

• It's acceptable for women to wear pants, but skirts or dresses are best. It's considered obscene for a woman to show her legs. Never wear tight or low-cut outfits.

• In cities, casual wear is acceptable. Women may wear pants, tank tops, and any loose-fitting clothing, but not miniskirts. In the mostly Muslim north, women should wear skirts that reach below the knees and should not wear pants unless riding a motorcycle.

• Men need not wear ties at most restaurants.

• Both men and women should dress conservatively and elegantly when doing business in Dakar, where there is still a great French influence.

• On Friday, a Muslim holy day, Muslims wear the traditional dress, called the *boubou*, a long, white, flowing garment. Some Muslims wear the *boubou* regularly, while others wear Western clothing.

• Neither men nor women should wear shorts outside a private home.

• As a visitor, don't wear traditional dress. Local people will think you strange.

• At the beach, bikinis are acceptable for women. Some French resorts have topless beaches.

• Don't act shocked if you see bare-breasted Senegalese women or women wearing just a bra and skirt.

• If you are a white woman, don't wear your hair in cornrows. It's considered disrespectful to black Senegalese women, and you may be harassed.

MEALS

Hours and Food

Breakfast: About 7:00 A.M. In cities people have French bread and café au lait. In rural areas, there will be millet and a sauce that is left over from the previous night's dinner. Rural Senegalese drink coffee made from a tea leaf with Nescafé and condensed milk added. Another beverage is *quinqueliba,* a traditional Senegalese herb tea.

Some people breakfast at the coffee ladies' stands on the street. One side of the stand has coffee, tea, and cocoa—beverages that are served *very* sweet—and the other side has fresh bread, which the vendor cuts and spreads with butter.

Lunch: Between noon and 2:00 P.M. The traditional lunch is *ceeb u jenn* (pronounced **cheb**-oo jenn). (For a description, see

"Specialties" below.) Another popular dish in rural areas is *yassa,* chicken with onions and (sometimes) olives.

After lunch, three rounds of very sweet tea are served in small glasses. Each round of tea has a different flavor. Sometimes one glass is passed around the group, and everyone drinks from it. Sometimes each person has an individual glass. The whole ceremony takes about an hour.

Dinner: About 8:00 P.M. Dishes are the same as those at lunch.

• Throughout the day, Senegalese snack on peanuts.

• Mutton, a common meat, is the standard dish at ceremonies, such as naming· ceremonies, at which sheep are slaughtered.

• A side dish at every lunch and dinner is spicy pepper oil.

• In the north, the base of all meals is ground millet, often served with grilled meat and fish.

• Common beverages are water, Coca-Cola, orange soda, and tonic water. The traditional beverage is *bisap* (bee-sahp), a red drink made from hibiscus flowers. Since it contains tap water, travelers should avoid it. From the tamarind comes another drink, *dakkhar* (dah-**chahr**—the "ch" as in the word *loch*). It's the refreshment featured at ceremonies such as weddings.

• In some homes, you'll be offered alcoholic beverages.

• In rural areas, if you don't want your coffee sweet, ask for it without sugar, because people routinely add sweetened condensed milk.

Table Manners

• If invited to a meal in a home, arrive at least 30 minutes late.

• Note that men and women usually eat separately, even though they may be in the same room.

• Seating arrangements vary. In cities, there is most often a table, while in the countryside stools and mats are used. If you are sitting on a mat on the floor, remove your shoes.

• At the beginning of the meal, a bowl, soap, and a towel will be brought around. Wash your hands, and pass the bowl on to the next person.

• Watch how your host eats, and imitate him. Sometimes there will be individual plates and silverware; sometimes a common bowl from which one eats with the right hand, and sometimes a common bowl and silverware for each person. Even if the Senegalese are eating with the right hand, they often provide a large soup spoon for a guest.

• Expect bowls of food to be brought to the table with a plastic cover or a calabash to keep the flies off. Wait for your host to remove the cover. Never do it yourself.

• The host or elders will divide up the fish and vegetables in the center and place choice morsels in front of each diner.

• Follow the Senegalese custom of dropping fish bones on the floor.

• Note that only one dish is served at a meal. For a large group, there will be several bowls, all containing the same dish.

• If the group is eating from a common bowl, all diners have unmarked "sections" of it. Don't reach into another person's area of the bowl. If your host doesn't know you well, you'll be given your own bowl and won't have to eat from the common bowl.

• Use *only* your right hand. If two hands are necessary to break the meat, two people do the breaking with their right hands.

• To eat, gather rice, meat, and sauce, and form it into a ball against the side of the bowl. Squeeze it until it's compact, and eat. Don't start to form another ball while there is still food in your mouth.

• When you've finished, clean off your part of the bowl with your hand, lick your hand, and get up and wash it.

• Remember that it's impolite to look at the face of someone who is still eating, but you may sit down again and speak to others who have finished.

• Traditionally, Senegalese talk very little while they are eating.

• In some areas, especially poorer ones, women pour a lot of oil onto the food to give it more substance. Some people like it; those who don't, take rice or millet and *squeeze* to get the oil out. (It's not considered rude.)

• Expect to be pushed to eat and eat until the communal bowl is empty. Your hosts will be very pleased if you eat a lot. However, you should leave a little food in your bowl or in your section of the communal bowl to show that you're really full.

• Never eat and run. It's insulting to leave right after a meal.

Eating Out

In Dakar, you'll find French, Belgian, American, Vietnamese, Lebanese, Italian, and Senegalese restaurants in all price ranges. There are also good pastry/ice cream shops, most of which are open until midnight. Other large cities will probably have a few good French restaurants; the rest will be Senegalese. In towns where you wait for public transportation, food may be available in small restaurants that are part of a house.

• Expect to see menus posted outside most restaurants. Even inexpensive restaurants usually provide a handwritten list of dishes with prices.

• The national dish, *ceeb u jenn,* may be listed as *riz au poisson* (rice with fish) on restaurant menus. The best versions of the dish will be at *ceeb* "joints" (called *gargotes* in French). They are in unmarked courtyards where you sit on a bench and eat *ceeb u jenn* out of plastic bowls.

• In restaurants, *ceeb u jenn* is served in individual bowls, whereas in homes there is just one communal bowl.

• To get the waiter's attention, say "*Garçon.*"

• If you are invited to a restaurant by a Senegalese, don't offer to pay.

Specialties: Senegal's national dish is *ceeb u jenn,* which means "rice with fish" in Wolof. The fish is a species of grouper; a stuffing is made with parsley, garlic, scallions, hot peppers, salt, black peppercorns, and bouillon cubes, all of which have been pounded into a paste. The accompanying vegetables vary with the season but may include cabbage, turnips, carrots, eggplant, okra, manioc, squash, and *jakatou* (a member of the eggplant family with a bitter taste). The fish and vegetables are stewed in a huge cauldron in a sauce made of onions, peanut oil, tomato paste, dried fish, tamarind seeds, white sorrel flowers, and red hot pepper.

When the stew is ready, rice is spread in a large, shallow bowl, with the fish and vegetables arranged artistically in the center. The browned crispy rice from the bottom of the cooking pot, considered a delicacy, is placed along the rim of the bowl, along with wedges of lime to squeeze over the fish.

Other specialties: *Yassa,* a dish served to show special honor to a guest, is made of chicken, rice, garlic, onions, chili peppers, and soy sauce; it is put in a bowl in the center of a cloth on the floor. *Mafe* (mah-**fay**), a chicken peanut stew, is composed of a chicken, cut into pieces, which is cooked with peanut oil, onions, tomatoes, peanut butter, cabbage, sweet potatoes, carrots, turnips, okra, and chili pepper. *Domada* (domah-**dah**) is fish, chicken, or beef in a sauce, served with boiled rice. *L'assiette des assiettes* (literally, "the dish of dishes") is an appetizer of white fish on black-eyed peas.

• Very common are kola nuts, a mild stimulant also used medicinally for nausea. Wash them, cut them open, and share them with others in your group. Some people swallow them; others spit them out after chewing them.

HOTELS

• At the best hotels, expect cable TV, plenty of hot water, maid service, telexes, fax machines, and conference rooms.

TIPPING

- Restaurants: You don't have to leave a tip, but if you wish to, give between 20 cents and $1.00 U.S.
- Porters: Give the equivalent of 40 cents to $1.00 U.S.
- Taxi drivers: No tip is necessary.
- Hotel room attendants: The equivalent of $1.00 U.S. per day.
- Household help in a private home: Give a gift such as makeup or perfume.
- In the countryside, cigarettes are regarded as a form of currency, so you can tip with a pack of cigarettes.

PRIVATE HOMES

- Note that people drop in on one another all the time, especially in villages. Senegalese even enjoy having people drop in at mealtime. If you drop in at mealtime and don't stay to share a meal, you have insulted your Senegalese host.
- Realize that in villages the concept of privacy does not exist.
- If you wish to go sightseeing on your own, your hosts won't be offended.
- If the family doesn't have household help, show yourself to be a considerate guest by making your own bed and offering to help set and clear the table. (In families without servants, chores are usually delegated to the youngest children.)
- Expect bathing habits to vary with the seasons. In December and January, buckets of water will be heated in the morning. Pour the water over yourself in the

bathroom, where there will be a drain in the floor. In other months, water won't be heated, because the weather is so hot.

• Remember that toilets may be in a separate room.

Gifts: If you come to a meal, follow the custom of bringing coffee or tea and sugar or pastry from one of the hundreds of French bakeries in the cities.

• Don't bring alcoholic beverages as a gift, since many people are Muslim and don't drink.

• From abroad, bring men and women watches, jeans, or sweaters. Men also like Swiss army knives. Women enjoy receiving earrings, cosmetics, or perfume. Teenagers appreciate cassettes with American pop singers, such as Bruce Springsteen and Whitney Houston.

• In villages, consider giving kola nuts. A chief will be flattered by receiving these nuts, readily available in markets. One kilo is about the right amount.

• In villages, both sexes enjoy receiving clothes. Women also appreciate jewelry, good hand cream, and nail polish.

BUSINESS

Hours

Businesses: Monday through Friday, 8:30 A.M. to 12:00 noon and 2:30 to 6:00 P.M.

Banks: 9:00 to 11:30 A.M. and 2:30 to 4:00 P.M.

Government Offices: Monday through Friday, 8:00 A.M. to noon and 2:30 to 6:00 P.M.

Stores: 8:00 A.M. to noon and 3:00 to 7:00 P.M.

Money

• The unit of currency is the West African Franc, abbreviated CFA (say-**fah**).

• Coins: 5, 10, 25, 50, and 100 CFA.

• Notes (Bills): 500, 1000, 5,000 and 10,000 CFA.

• Good restaurants and hotels accept credit cards.

Business Practices

• A good source for business contacts is the Chambre de Commerce in Dakar.

• Note that business is conducted in both French and English, if the businesspeople have studied in the U.S. or England.

• Make appointments from abroad a week in advance. Senegalese are accommodating and will try to fit you in. Schedule appointments in the morning, the coolest time of day.

• Check a Muslim calendar to see when Ramadan occurs, and avoid making business appointments during that time, as people will be very tired from fasting. (Remember that the overwhelming portion of Senegal's population is Muslim.)

• Expect to find faxes available everywhere. Even in villages, you will find shops that are comparable to North America's alternatives to the post office. However, photocopying is not widely available; when it is, it is expensive.

• Be aware that people who have lived in the West tend to be more punctual than other Senegalese.

• Be patient. If the Senegalese businesspeople don't know you, it will take some time for them to trust you.

• Always chat before getting down to business.

• Never show anger, no matter how frustrated or provoked you may feel.

• If you're dealing with government officials, be prepared for many meetings and calls. Ministry officials make little money, but they wield power and can be assertive.

• Note that there are women in powerful positions in Senegal. Feel free to send a businesswoman from your company. However, women must remember not to behave in a manner that could be construed as aggressive.

• Don't be surprised if your business counterpart entertains you at home. To reciprocate, ask the Senegalese to recommend a restaurant, and treat her/him to a meal there.

HOLIDAYS AND SPECIAL OCCASIONS

• The following holidays are celebrated in Senegal: New Year's Day (January 1); Confederation Senegambia (February 1); National Day (April 4); Easter Monday; Labor Day (May 1); Whit Monday; Assumption Day (August 15); All Saints' Day (November 1); Christmas (December 25).

• The following holidays very with the Muslim calendar: Ramadan; Mohammed's birthday; Tabaski.

• Mohammed's birthday, called Gamu, is celebrated on the eleventh day of the third Muslim month. Prayer vigils are held at night.

TRANSPORTATION

Public Transportation

• Keep in mind that there are several levels of public transportation: (1) the best—white station wagons, which accommodate about seven people; (2) next level—the *car rapide,* a van, which takes 15 people; (3) next level—a blue bus, crowded with many, many people; (4) the bottom—pickup trucks with two benches on the side, which don't move until they are filled. These trucks don't run on a schedule and often break down. Even though there are set rates, the driver may try to charge foreigners more. Ask a Senegalese in advance what the fare should be.

• Expect to find regular taxis in Dakar. If you would prefer to have the taxi to yourself, pay the fare that would be charged to several persons sharing the cab.

- Note that the *cars rapides* run both in cities and between cities.
- Consider taking a bus. The bus service in Senegal is excellent.
- Avoid taking trains within the country. They are *very* slow.
- If you're going to Mali, by all means take the Senegalese train there. It is new and is one of the best in Africa. You can reserve seats in first class, which is air-conditioned. Seats in second class can't be reserved, so arrive early. The train offers a dining car and *couchettes* (berths) in compartments to be shared by two people.
- Bring your own toilet paper or tissues.
- If you wish to fly within Senegal, go in person to the Air Senegal office to book your ticket. The airline will not accept reservations by phone.
- When you arrive at the airport, many people will try to grab your bags to carry. Either settle on a price first, or carry your own.

Driving

- Bring an International Driver's License.
- Try to avoid driving in Dakar. The city is so crowded that driving is difficult.

- Expect to find paved roads very good, but if you go off the main roads in the rainy season (May–September), you'll have problems unless you have four-wheel drive.
- When driving outside the city, be careful of animals on the road.
- Realize that people often drive recklessly, which results in frequent accidents.
- Don't be surprised to be stopped, even when you haven't done anything wrong. An "on-the-spot" fine, which is really a bribe, may be assessed.

LEGAL MATTERS, HEALTH, AND SAFETY

- Don't buy the ivory that some Senegalese will try to sell you out of suitcases. Bringing it into the U.S. is illegal.
- Note that you need not register with the police.

• Stick to bottled water; it's available everywhere.

• Be cautious in Dakar. To foil the many pickpockets, wear a money belt.

• In Dakar, don't be surprised to be besieged by people who either are trying to steal your money or sell you things.

• Never wear expensive jewelry; stick to costume jewelry.

• Don't take valuables if you go to a beach, as petty thefts are common.

• Cities are much more dangerous than villages. Even when walking with a group in a city, don't go down dark streets, especially at night, because you risk being mugged.

• Women should never walk alone at night and should be prepared to be harassed. Taxi drivers especially may become very rude, asking if you have boyfriends, etc. One woman responded that she had seven husbands and could not deal with another one. She defused the harassment with a joke—much better than anger.

KEY PHRASES

The following phrases are in Wolof.

English	*Wolof Pronunciation*
Good morning	ya-**man**-gah fah-**nin**
Good evening	ya-**man**-gah **yen**-lou
Good-bye	mahn-gah-**dem**
Mr.	seh-**rign**-bee
Mrs. and Miss	**soch**-nah see*
Please	boo-cheh-lah-**neh***
Thank you	jair-ruh-**jehf**

*The "ch" in these phrases is pronounced as the "ch" in "loch."

You're welcome	nee-o-**ko** bok
Yes	**wow**
No	**deh**-det
Excuse me	bahl mah
I don't understand	**chow**-mah
I don't speak Wolof	deh-**goo**-mah **woh**-lof
Does anyone speak English?	ndahch **ahm**-nah koo fee lahk ahn-gleh **day**-gay?*

Here are commonly used French phrases.

English	*French Pronunciation*
Good day	bawn-**zhoor**
Good evening	bawn-**swahr**
Please	seel-voo-**pleh**
Thank you	mehr-**see**
You're welcome	de ree-en
Yes	wee
No	nawn
Mr., Sir	meh-**syeu**
Mrs., Madame	mah-**dahm**
Miss	mahd-mwah-**zehl**
Excuse me	ex-kyou-zay **mwah**
Good-bye	o reh-**vwahr**
I don't understand	zhe ne kawn-prahn **pah**
I don't speak French	zhe ne pahrl pah frawn-**seh**
Do you speak English?	pahr-lay voo ahn-**gleh**?

SOUTH AFRICA

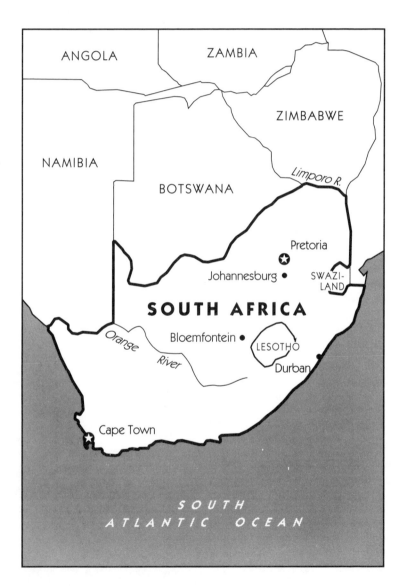

Few people have summed up the grandeur and sadness of South Africa so well as travel writer Judith Carter:

> *I doubt you can travel in South Africa without the urge to peer into the future tugging relentlessly at every turn. It is a place of indisputable beauty; a land that has yielded some of the earth's greatest riches, fuelling greed and vanity as men dug and died for gold and diamonds. The imprint of European settlers lies everywhere—great and grandiose schemes that rarely honoured indigenous species. Officially, the oppression of one group of people by another is over, but the legacy is a never-ending horizon.*

Those of us moved by the beauty of South Africa can but hope that the Nobel Peace Prize awarded jointly to Nelson Mandela and F.W. de Klerk portends a future of harmony in one of the world's most spectacularly handsome countries.

GREETINGS

• Remember that an "African handshake" is used between blacks and whites and blacks and blacks. Shake hands and, without letting go, slip your hand around the other person's thumb; then go back to the traditional handshake. Whites do not use this handshake with other whites.

• Afrikaaners and whites shake hands when introduced: men and men, men and women, and women and women.

• Good friends of opposite sexes: men kiss women on one cheek. Men greet close male friends with a handshake or a hug.

• In greeting men in a business setting, women should nod or shake hands.

• Be sure to use the title "Doctor" or "Professor" when appropriate; address a lawyer as "Mister." Refer to an advocate who pleads in the Supreme Court as "Advocate" with the last name.

• Use first names only after a South African does.

• Don't be surprised if blacks don't rise when introduced. It's a sign of respect not to be higher than a man of higher status. This gesture does not apply when women are being greeted.

CONVERSATION

• Note that English and Afrikaans are the official languages. Most South Africans speak one of the two languages, and often both. Over six million people (24.5% of the population) speak Zulu. The language next in popularity is Xhosa.

• Afrikaaners in urban areas speak English; in rural white areas, they usually speak only Afrikaans. In black regions, people speak their native language first and English second.

• Good subjects for conversation: the weather, the beauty of South Africa; the other person's occupation; advice as to what you as a foreigner should see and do.

• Don't ask personal questions (e.g., whether a person is mar-

ried). South Africans, like the English, are reserved.

• Never criticize the country and its people. South Africans have been subjected to so much criticism regarding apartheid that they are very touchy. People who live outside cities are especially sensitive to cricitism. Be careful not to compare South Africa to another country.

• Avoid discussing the political situation and ethnic differences.

• Don't compliment people in public, but it's okay to do so in private.

• Feel free to use the word "white," but don't use the term "non-white" to refer to other groups in the country.

• If you hear the term "brown Afrikaaner," the reference is to a colored person (one of mixed race).

• Never use the word "kaffir" to refer to blacks. It is a racially abhorrent term used during the apartheid era.

• Note that "Asian" is an apartheid classification, referring to anyone with roots in Asia. Many Chinese and Indians find the term derogatory because it doesn't take into account Asia's diversity. Refer to persons by the country of their origin.

• Other offensive terms to avoid: "coolie," referring to Indians; "hotnot," in reference to people of mixed race.

• Don't swear, unless you know someone well. South Africa has a tradition of puritanical behavior. If you hear people swearing a great deal, it may be that they have heard the English words and don't know their meanings.

• Be aware that the phrase "just now" means "in a short while"—not "immediately."

• Be aware that it's a sign of disrespect for blacks to look another person in the eye.

TELEPHONES

• South Africa has the best telephone system in all of Africa.

• Expect to find public phones everywhere—on the streets, in post offices, in department stores, in restaurants. However, oftentimes phones in major cities don't work, because they have been vandalized.

• To make a call from a public phone, deposit 30 cents local currency for three minutes. You'll hear a beep when the money runs out. Deposit more money *immediately*, or you will be cut off. (You'll find instructions for calling on the phones.)

• If you need an operator, you'll find some who speak English and some who speak Afrikaans.

• If you will be using public phones frequently, buy a telephone card at a post office.

• You can make an international call from your hotel, but it will be expensive. For more reasonable rates, make your call from the post office.

• Before you ask to make a call from a private home, recall that people are charged for even local calls.

• In an emergency, for police, fire, or ambulance, call 999.

IN PUBLIC

• Keep in mind that manners in South Africa are not so formal as those in England, but not so relaxed as those in the United States.

• Note that it's customary for an African male to precede a woman through a door.

• Ask permission of those around you before you smoke.

• Try to follow the African custom of giving and receiving with the right hand. Traditional people may give or receive with both hands.

• Two gestures to remember: (1) the raised fist of the right hand is a symbol of black power; (2) the "V" sign with palm facing toward you is obscene.

• Bargain in markets and in black or Indian shops, but don't bargain in white shops, where prices are fixed.

• Look for public bathrooms in city parks, in malls, hotels, restaurants, cinemas, shops, and along the beachfront. They are labeled in two languages: *Dames*/Women; *Here*/Men. In the countryside, toilet paper and paper towels may not be available. Public washrooms don't have attendants.

DRESS

• Realize that South Africans tend to dress fashionably and conservatively in terms of both style and color.

• For casual dress in cities, both women and men may wear shorts or jeans. However, the Boer farmers in rural communities are very conservative. In those areas, women should not bare shoulders or wear tops that are low-cut. In other areas, people are used to seeing women in halter tops and sleeveless dresses.

• For viewing game, wear jeans and a windbreaker.

• When invited to a meal in a home during the summer (northern hemisphere's winter), ask how you should dress, because sometimes people sit around the pool in bathing suits and eat outdoors. When eating is indoors, both men and women may wear jeans or pants and a shirt.

• To an ordinary restaurant, men should wear pants and a shirt; women should wear pants or a dress. To elegant restaurants, men should wear a suit, and women a dress.

• For business appointments, men should wear suits and ties, and women should wear dresses or suits. Africans tend to wear colored shirts with suits. In summer, the business "uniform" is often the khaki shirt and Bermuda shorts.

• Note that there are some beaches where women can be topless—but never completely nude. Check first.

• Expect to find changing cabins at beaches.

• To the theater, men should wear a suit, and women should wear dresses.

• If black tie is in order, the invitation to the event will so state. Formal dress is usual for opening nights at the opera, a wedding, or a special gala event.

• Note that blacks wear traditional dress for ceremonial occasions.

• Remember that winter in South Africa is between June and August. Homes aren't prepared for cold weather, and central heating is rare. Dress warmly inside.

MEALS

Hours and Foods

Breakfast: Sometime between 8:00 and 9:30 A.M. Usually a hearty meal, breakfast offers cereal (porridge), bacon, sausage, eggs, toast or rolls, and tea or coffee.

Lunch: Normally between 1:00 and 2:00 P.M. A light meal of salad, cold meats, fruit, and beer or soda.

Dinner: Families eat at 7:00 P.M. Dinner parties usually begin at 8:00 P.M. Dinner is often a barbecue. Common dishes: steak, fish, or chicken; salad served with the main course; desserts; wine and beer with the meals and coffee and liqueurs afterward.

• At 11:00 A.M. and 4:00 P.M., people have tea with sandwiches, scones, cookies (which may be referred to as "biscuits," as is the English custom) or cake. In work places there are no formal coffee breaks, but people often go out for coffee at 10:00 A.M. and for tea at 4:00 P.M. More often, people have tea at their desk.

• Note that most people don't consider a meal complete without a meat dish. In the winter, because of the hunting season, venison and warthog (similar to wild boar) are popular.

• Among Afrikaaners, *biltong* (the equivalent of American beef jerky) is favored. Usually made of venison, *biltong* consists of strips of meat that are salted, spiced, and dried in the sun.

• Venison—marinated, grilled, or roasted—served with vegetables is a favorite dish.

• The mainstay of the black South African diet is corn, called *mealies,* usually eaten as a porridge. With curdled milk, this pounded corn porridge is the traditional meal. For ceremonial occasions, slaughtered cattle, goats, and sheep are cooked with the corn porridge.

• The *Braaivleis* (barbecue), often shortened to *Braai,* is a common form of entertaining at either lunch or dinner. Children are included in invitations. The meal will consist of different meats or fish, with salads, rolls, and special sauces. The meats are usually mutton, steak, and *boerewors* (heavily spiced sausages), and occasionally venison. At a traditional *Braai,* you'll be offered *mieliepap,* a stiff porridge made from maize, similar to Italian polenta.

Beverages: Before lunch, cold beer may be offered.

• Before dinner, drinks will be served. Wine is becoming more common than mixed drinks; sometimes champagne will be served. Wine will probably accompany dinner. After dinner will come liqueurs.

• Be careful if you're offered one of these home brews: *mapoer* or *witblitz* (white lightning). Similar to schnapps, both of these illegally brewed beverages are high in alcohol content.

• A local drink, called "cane," is a sugarcane distillate. Although it has little taste, it's used as a mixer—e.g., cane and Coke.

• Expect to find many varieties of beer, since almost all South Africans drink it. One variety is a traditional African beer, made from sorghum, called *maheu* (mahe-oo). This thick, sour brew— low in alcohol and high in nutrition—is an acquired taste. In urban areas, it's produced commercially; in rural areas, it's home brewed.

• If you're pressured to drink and don't want to, explain that you are abstaining for medical reasons.

Table Manners

• Be on time when invited to dinner.

• Let your host seat you. The most important guests will be placed next to the host and hostess.

• A person offering a *serviette* is asking if you want a napkin.

• Note that South Africans eat European style—fork in the left hand, knife between the thumb and forefinger of the right hand. They won't expect you to imitate them.

• Expect your hostess or a servant to serve onto individual plates from platters on a sideboard. Help yourself only at a buffet.

• Don't start eating until the host or hostess picks up his/her fork.

• Don't feel obliged to have a second helping or to finish everything on your plate.

• To indicate that you have finished, place your utensils vertically on the plate.

• Remember that it's acceptable to smoke after the meal, but not between courses. Ask your host or hostess before lighting up. Some people go outside after dinner to smoke in order not to bother others.

• Stay for about an hour after the meal. Leave a dinner party at 11:00 or 11:30 P.M.; a small, quiet dinner at about 10:30 P.M.; a pre-dinner drink party, no later than 7:00 or 7:30 P.M.; a cocktail party, between 7:00 and 8:00 P.M.

• If you invite people to a meal, construct your menu without pork if any guests are Jewish or Muslim, and remember that Muslims don't drink alcohol.

Eating Out

• Note that nightlife in South Africa ends earlier than in Europe. Most restaurants will not seat people after 10:00 P.M.

• Reserve in advance, especially for weekends. Always reserve for the best restaurants. When you reserve at an elegant restaurant, inquire if there's a dress code for men. Some require men to wear a jacket and tie (although women may wear elegant pants).

• Many restaurants post menus in the windows.

• Check the government rating

of a restaurant before choosing it. The ratings run from one to five stars.

• If you're looking for a pub snack, try a *prego* roll; the crispy roll with a steak—similar to a steak sandwich—is of Portuguese origin.

• Be aware that *cafes* resemble convenience stores. They sell eggs, bread, milk, canned foods, soft drinks, and magazines— but not liquor. Some offer "fast food" sandwiches, and some have tables where you can sit and enjoy coffee, tea, and snacks. *Cafes* are open from 7:00 A.M. to 10:00 P.M. every day, including holidays.

• If you're interested in trying game dishes—e.g., crocodile steak, elephant stew—seek out one of the restaurants that specializes in game.

• Wait to be seated; don't join others at a table, except in a crowded fast-food restaurant.

• Be aware that in expensive restaurants, only the host receives a menu with prices.

• To attract the waiter's attention, raise your hand.

• In better restaurants, pay at the table. In less elegant establishments, pay at the cashier's desk as you leave.

• Most bars remain open from 10:00 A.M. to 11:00 P.M., Monday through Saturday. On Sunday, alcoholic beverages are usually served only with meals.

• Note that some restaurants have a complete liquor license, and others can serve only wine, beer, and a few liqueurs. To those with no license, you may bring your own drinks. Even if a restaurant has a license, you may bring your own liquor and pay a corkage fee. Some restaurants frown upon this practice—and will make that displeasure very clear to you.

• If you wish to buy liquor, go to a "bottle store," where you can purchase all kinds of liquor on Monday through Friday between 9:00 A.M. and 5:00 P.M. and on Saturday between 9:00 A.M. and 1:00 P.M. Most supermarkets sell beer and wine. Liquor isn't sold on Sunday.

• The official drinking age is 18, and there are fines for people selling liquor to minors.

• Women should recall that they are not welcome in some pubs. Look around when you enter. If you don't see other women, it's probably wise to leave.

Specialties

• Either in a private home or a restaurant, you may find *potjiekos* (pot food). A three-legged iron pot is tightly packed with raw vegetables, meat, and fish, which are cooked together for a long time.

• Popular seafood dishes are crayfish, oysters, clams, and mussels. They are flown in fresh to inland areas.

• Cape Malay specialties: *bredies* (a meat and vegetable stew, whose base may be tomato, quince, pumpkin, or cabbage); *bobotie* (baked ground meat with spices and sometimes dried fruit); *pinangkerrie* (meat curry with tamarind); *denningvleis* (meat with bay leaves and tamarind); *sosaties* (similar to shish kebab); *smoorsnoek* (a snack made of a smoked, firm-fleshed fish).

• Popular side dishes: yellow rice (flavored with turmeric or saffron and raisins); chutney and *atchars* (pickles); tangerine peel and pickled peaches. Two sweets are tipsy tart (a brandy tart), and *koeksisters* (sweet rolls). Curries are accompanied by a drink made of sour milk with a slice of orange rind.

• The major Afrikaaner specialty is *biltong,* made from strips of beef or game which have been spiced, salted, and dried. Another favorite is cooked green maize, which is like corn on the cob.

• Specialties in black areas: sorghum porridge, served with milk and sugar at breakfast; *mopani* worms, dried and eaten as snacks; *mealie,* (corn) on the cob, roasted over charcoal and available at the end of summer and beginning of winter. It's sold on the street near bus and train stations.

• Other specialties, found throughout the country: *kingklip,* a firm-fleshed fish, usually served fried; *waterblommetjie bredie,* mutton stew with water hyacinth flowers (which have a slight peppery flavor) and white wine.

HOTELS

• Note that the South African Tourism Board rates hotels; however, there are also deluxe small inns, private lodges, and game lodges, which are not rated. The following are the categories and amenities:

• *1-star:* Good, with private bathrooms (which includes bathtub and toilet) for half the rooms and showers (shower plus toilet) in the other half. They must provide a 12-hour service of light snacks and alcoholic drinks.

• *2-star:* Very good, with bathrooms in 60% of the rooms and showers in the others. Heating, radios, light snacks, and alcoholic drinks must be available 14 hours a day.

• *3-star:* Excellent, with bathrooms in 75% of the bedrooms and showers in the rest. They will have carpeting, heating, radio, plugs for razors, à la carte meals for six hours a day, 18-hour room service, 24-hour telephone service, color TV in a public room (most have TVs in every room), and one function room.

• *4-star:* Outstanding, with bathrooms in 90% of the rooms and showers in the rest. Rooms have air-conditioning; heating; plugs for razors; radios; 24-hour phone service; TV in 50% of the bedrooms; valet service from 7:00 A.M. to 9:00 P.M., à la carte meals for seven hours a day; 24-hour room service for snacks, light meals, and alcoholic beverages; 24-hour reception; full-time beauty salon; transport; two conference rooms; and secretarial service.

• *5-star:* The very best, with at least 5% of the accommodations suites and 95% of the rooms with baths and showers. There are four-channel radios, TVs, heat, air-conditioning, 24-hour room service for light meals and alcoholic drinks, full meals from 7:00 A.M. to 9:00 P.M., valet service, 24-hour reception, beauty salons for men and women, two restaurants with à la carte menus, and conference rooms.

• Expect major hotels to have fax machines and telex services available for guests.

• If you'll be traveling off-season (summer in the U.S. is winter in South Africa), ask about discounted rates available at many hotels.

• Ask to be sure that your hotel follows the custom of including breakfast in your room rate.

• Be prepared to produce your passport when you check in.

• Be sure to put your valuables in the hotel's safe-deposit box.

• Near favorite tourist attractions and resorts, you'll find bed-and-breakfast accommodations available in private homes. Staying in a B&B is a good way to meet South Africans and to see some lovely homes. The idea is fairly new in South Africa. Check with the newly organized Bed & Breakfast Association for accommodations.

• If you would like to camp, possibly in one of the many campsites around the country (including Kruger National Park), keep in mind that you can rent a camper or RV in most cities.

• Take a flashlight to use outdoors in Kruger National Park. The area where you'll stay is secured by a fence. The park is open from 6:00 A.M. to 6:30 P.M. If after 6:30 P.M. you're found outside the fenced-in area, you'll be fined. Within the park, there are fully equipped guest cottages and huts with kitchenette and shower or bath.

TIPPING

• Tip 10% at restaurants.
• Give porters $1.00 U.S. per bag.
• Tip taxi drivers 10% to 15% of the fare.
• Leave hotel room attendants $5.00 U.S. per week.
• Tip cloakroom attendants 50 cents U.S.

• Don't tip ushers or gas station attendants.

PRIVATE HOMES

• Be aware that people often entertain at home. The style is usually casual. Offer to contribute something, such as wine, beer, or a dessert, a donation your hosts will appreciate. You will usually have drinks, dinner, and conversation. If the central event will be tennis, bridge, or swimming in a pool, you'll be told when the invitation is issued.

• Sometimes people will entertain you at a club (golf club, bowling club, etc.).

• Don't be surprised to be invited to drop in anytime or to come over to have drinks. Such invitations are usually sincere, but be sure to confirm them a day or two ahead. (Call on Friday and ask if it would be convenient for you to come by at 4:00 P.M. on Sunday.) If you arrive without calling, you may be embarrassed, as it may be the children's bath time or dinnertime.

• After you and your host have agreed on a time, be sure to be punctual.

• Since South Africans are early risers, don't stay after 11:00 P.M. on a weekend. Leave earlier on a weeknight.

• Although hosts in the United States usually walk guests to the door, your South African host will probably walk you to your car.

• Should you make a long-distance call, ask the operator to inform you of the charges, and pay your host for the call.

• Note that there is constant hot water, so it's okay to bathe daily. However, ask first, because there are droughts during some periods in certain parts of the country.

• Feel free to make independent plans, although your host family will show you around if you would like.

• If you're staying with a family, offer to help with the chores unless there are servants.

• If there's a household helper and you ask her to perform a service such as doing your laundry, tip her.

• Because of the country's inflation, your hosts will appreciate it if you take them to a restaurant and/or go food shopping with them and pay for the groceries. (You might say that you want to see a South African store, go along for the shopping, and then pay.) You could also bring the family an occasional treat, such as a cake or a bottle of wine.

• Both white and black families may have servants. A good way to thank household help for their service is to give them a gift when you leave—e.g., a T-shirt or a CD. Be discreet when you give the gift, in case your host or hostess might not approve. If you'd prefer, give money.

• When invited to a meal, bring wine, chocolates, or flowers.

BUSINESS

Hours

Businesses: Monday through Friday, 8:00 or 8:30 A.M. to 5:00 P.M. A few start at 9:00 A.M. and close at 6:00 P.M., but no switchboard is open after 5:00 P.M.

Government Offices: Monday through Friday, 7:15 or 7:30 A.M. to 3:30 or 4:30 P.M.

Banks: Monday through Friday, 9:00 A.M. to 3:30 P.M., and Saturday, 9:00 to 11:00 A.M.

Shops: Monday through Friday, 8:30 A.M. to 5:00 P.M., and Saturday, 8:30 A.M. to 1:00 P.M.

• Almost everything, including banks and post offices, closes between 1:00 and 2:00 P.M., especially in small towns and villages.

• Major supermarkets remain open on Saturday afternoon, and some open on Sunday mornings as well.

Money

• The unit of currency is the Rand (R), made up of 100 cents (c).

• Coins: 1, 2, 5, 10, 20, and 50 cents; 1 and 2 Rand.

• Notes (Bills): 5, 10, 20 and 50 Rand.

• Realize that there are two exchange rates—one for investors, called the financial rate, which is discounted 20%, and the commercial rate, which is for tourists.

• Exchange money at a bank for the most favorable rate. Hotels often change money, but the rate will be less advantageous.

• As a tourist, you can get a refund on the VAT (Value-Added Tax) at the airport when you leave. Ask stores for vouchers, and be sure to keep all receipts.

• Expect major credit cards to be welcomed in most stores, hotels, restaurants, and car rental agencies—but not in gas stations. Carry your passport or some other form of identification, in case proof of identity is required.

Business Practices

• To find a contact in South Africa, get in touch with the South African Chamber of Commerce and Industry in Johannasburg, the American Chamber of Commerce in Johannesburg, the U.S. Foreign Commercial Service at the American Consulate in Johannesburg, and the South African Trade Commission in Washington, D.C. Many times business contacts are made through word of mouth. In London, contact the Commercial Section of the South African Embassy. In Ottawa, contact the Commercial Section of the South African Embassy.

• From abroad, make appointments two months in advance. If someone is anxious to do business with you, only a short advance notice will be required. If your schedule will be tight, let your South African counterparts know; they will usually make themselves available at short notice.

• Avoid making appointments for the period between December 16 and January 12. That's South Africa's summer, and the country all but shuts down. Also avoid the week preceding Easter.

• Consult a calendar for the principal Jewish holidays, which change every year. South Africa has a sizable Jewish business community, and no business meetings will be scheduled on Jewish holidays.

• Schedule appointments at any time during the day. One time is no better than another.

• Note that computers, faxes, telexes, and photocopying facilities are widely available.

• Bring graphics and visual aids to enhance your probability of success.

• To an initial meeting, send someone fairly senior in your company's hierarchy. Negotiations will be easier, since decisions are made by the top people in South African companies.

• If a black African cannot meet with you because he has to go to a funeral, he may be gone for days. Tribal funerals and mourning usually last a long time. Africans in cities may journey to rural areas to bury a relative. In addition, don't think you're being "conned," if someone goes to his father's funeral on three different occasions. Blacks may refer to people as brother or father, even when no blood relationship is involved.

• Be sure to be punctual.

• Bring business cards printed in English, since English is widely spoken.

• Always greet people at length before getting down to business. When you walk into an office, begin a meeting, or go to a factory, ask the other person about his family, and wait for an answer. Never merely say "Hello" in greeting.

• Expect to be offered coffee and/or tea at a business meeting.

• After a brief period of personal conversation, discussion of business will begin.

• Note that personal relationships are important, and it may take a while to develop one. South African businesspeople tend to be cautious, because they have not been in the international business community for many years, and fear being exploited. They will need time to trust the integrity of a foreign businessperson.

• Don't expect hard bargaining. It isn't a part of South Africa's business culture, except in the Indian community. Leave a margin for yourself, but it need not be a wide one.

• Realize that members of the Indian business community are very shrewd and take a long time to make a deal.

• Be sure to obtain a written contract. Although verbal contracts can be enforced in court, the process can be time-consuming and expensive.

• Remember that business gifts are not common. If your relationship with a South African progresses to the point at which you want to give a gift, select a desk set, a good pen and pencil set, or a diary.

• Women should know that South Africa lags behind other industrialized countries in hiring women for senior management positions.

• Be prepared for chauvinism. Businesswomen may be referred to as "girls." In meetings, men frequently expect women—even their peers or superiors—to make tea. Women may also be intentionally excluded from discussions while decisions are made. If a North American businesswoman, high in the echelon of her firm, is sent to South Africa, she won't be subject to such male condescension. American women should not be overly aggressive in manner, or they won't be accepted.

Business Entertaining: While South Africans are very hospitable and often invite business acquaintances to their homes, the first time they entertain you will probably be in a restaurant or at lunch in a private club. Other popular methods of entertaining business colleagues: lunches, cocktail parties, dinners, and daytime sporting events.

• Expect a business lunch, which is a common form of entertaining, to last a long time. Spouses aren't included in business lunches.

• Business dinners are social events, and spouses are often included.

• Don't plan to reciprocate while you're in South Africa. It's not customary. Plan to entertain the South African when he/she comes to your country.

HOLIDAYS AND SPECIAL OCCASIONS

• South Africa observes the following holidays: New Year's Day (January 1); Good Friday; Easter Monday; Founder's Day (April 6—commemorating the arrival of Cape Colony founder Jan Van Riebieck from Holland in 1652); Ascension Day (40 days after Easter); Republic Day (May 31); Kruger Day (October 10—in honor of statesman and soldier Paul Kruger); Day of the Vow (December 16—the date on which white settlers were slaughtered by Zulus); Christmas (December 25); Day of Good Will (December 26).

TRANSPORTATION

Public Transportation

• Expect behavior on public transportation to be generally reserved, except after a rugby game, when there may be rowdiness.

• If you plan to use public transportation, always check at your hotel or with your hosts as to which areas may not be safe.

• A major source of income for blacks is the combi-taxi, a minibus, which seats 8 to 15 fairly comfortably, but sometimes as many as 20 people are packed in. They run on set routes but sometimes deviate a little. These taxis are patronized mainly by blacks, but anyone can take one. A young American traveler found them great for making contact with people. However, since they mainly shuttle blacks from the townships where they live to the town in which they work, you might find yourself in an area that isn't entirely safe.

• Note that there are intra-city and inter-city taxis. You'll have to ask which is which, because there are no signs.

• Private taxis take just one passenger. The cars are usually in better condition and more comfortable.

• Look for a sedan taxi (a private taxi) at major hotels and strategically located taxi ranks at major points in the cities. They usually cannot be hailed on the street. If you wish, ask a member of the hotel staff to phone for one. If you're going to visit a friend, ask the driver who takes you there for a card, so that you can phone for a taxi for the return journey. Sedan taxis are supposed to operate with a meter, but check to be sure that there is one before you get in the cab. If there is no meter, bargain about the fare.

• Don't plan to rely on buses for transportation. They run infrequently except during peak hours, and they cover few routes.

• Cape Town and Soweto have commuter trains. There are two classes, with smoking and non-smoking sections; neither class has food service. Buy your ticket in advance at the kiosk in the train station.

• When you arrive, check at the Government Tourist Office about buying a special pass. Discounts are offered on main line passenger trains for groups of four passengers in first class and six passengers in second class. Greyhound buses offer a 20% discount on Monday through Thursday for senior citizens (except during December and at other holiday periods). Translux buses offer a 5% discount.

• To experience train travel as it was in its "glory days," take the Blue Train. Its overnight accommodations range from luxury suites (Type A) to standard (Type D). Lunch, dinner, and breakfast are included in the fare. There are baths, showers, a lounge, a bar, and a dining room. The experience is like a journey in a five-star hotel. The Blue Train runs from Cape Town to Pretoria and back, with a stop in Johannesburg. You may need to reserve months in advance, because the Blue Train is regarded as one of the best trains in the world. (If you want to get yourself in the mood for your trip, read Agatha Christie's *The Mystery of the Blue Train*.)

• Note that regular long-distance trains have sleeping berths in first and second class. First class offers coupes (which are smaller than compartments and sleep two) and compartments (which sleep four). Second-class coupes and compartments accommodate three passengers, and third-class compartments take six passengers. Most long-distance trains have dining cars for cocktails, meals, or light refreshments and offer food and drink via corridor service.

• Major cities are connected by plane service.

• At South Africa's international airports, expect to be approached by porters with both hands held out in a cupped shape. The porters are not begging; the gesture is one of humility, signifying that the gift you may give me for carrying your bags will mean so much that I must hold it in two hands.

Driving

• Rent a car through one of the international car rental firms—Avis, Budget, Imperial—which you'll find in major cities and at most tourist spots. In some cities, there are local companies. Some rental firms provide four-wheel-drive vehicles for remote areas.

• Use your home country's driver's license, which is good for six months, provided that the license is in English and has your photo on it. Otherwise, you'll need an International Driver's License.

• Be aware that driving is on the left, as in England.

• Be sure to wear your seat belt. Both adults and children must buckle up.

• If you would like to hire a car with a driver, ask your hotel to make the arrangements.

• South Africa's main roads are excellent, and traffic is usually not heavy, except during peak holiday periods.

• Gas stations—called petrol filling stations—are plentiful on main and country roads. Hours are generally 7:00 A.M. to 6:00 P.M., but some are open 24 hours.

• Expect the speed limit in built-up areas to be 60 km (about 35 miles) per hour; on rural roads 100 kph (about 60 mph); on freeways 120 kph (about 72 mph). In some areas, different speed limits will be posted.

• Street signs are clear in towns, but countryside streets and roads are less well marked. Go the A.A. (the Automobile Association) for maps.

• Look for parking meters and signs to show where you can park, for how long you can park, and where you can't park. If there is no sign, parking is legal.

• If you're having a problem with directions, etc., go to the police station. The police are very helpful.

• DON'T drive after drinking. There are *very* heavy penalties for drunken driving—including arrest.

• Don't expect to pay an on-the-spot fine for a traffic violation. You'll be given a ticket to be paid at a Traffic Control Department or a police station.

• If you're driving in the countryside, beware of animals in the road.

• Be aware that it's illegal to make a U-turn.

LEGAL MATTERS, HEALTH, AND SAFETY

• Don't bring into the country any material that Customs officials might regard as pornographic. Such magazines as *Playboy* and *Penthouse* fall into that category. If you try to carry such publications into South Africa, Customs officials may give you a very hard time.

• Gambling is illegal, except in the independent homelands.

• Don't forget that malaria is a problem in the Lowveld area, where Kruger National Park and most private game parks are located. Start taking antimalarial pills at least one week prior to visiting that area.

• Don't swim in water holes, in streams, or in rivers. There's a danger of the parasitic disease bilharzia and of crocodiles.

• Feel free to drink the tap water in major cities. Fruits and vegetables are also safe.

• Beware of car-jackings and pickpocketing, even in the daytime.

• Keep in mind that street crime and pilfering from hotel rooms have increased in large cities.

• Don't walk around at night. Cape Town is a reasonably safe city, but no one lives in the city center, where there are many hotels. Streets are deserted at night.

• Stay away from demonstrations, however curious you may be.

TANZANIA

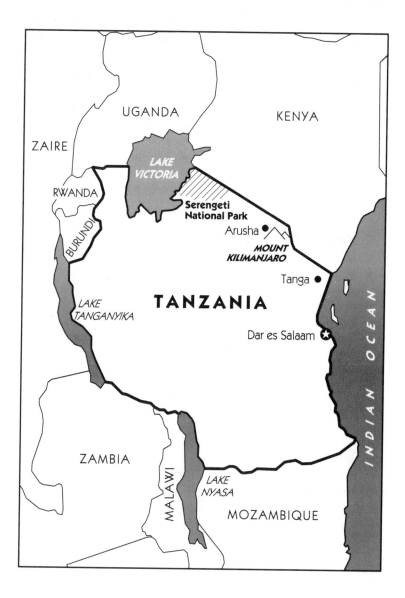

In Tanzania, one of the most famous questions in the English language was asked: "Dr. Livingstone, I presume?" Thus Henry Morgan Stanley ended his search for Dr. David Livingstone near Lake Tanganyika and passed into quotation history.

Almost a century later, Gregory Peck lay expiring in the shadow of Africa's highest mountain, Mount Kilimanjaro, in *The Snows of Kilimanjaro* (a film adapted from the Ernest Hemingway short story), as Susan Hayward looked helplessly on.

In addition to the continent's highest mountain, Tanzania boasts the world's second largest lake (Lake Victoria) and the world's second deepest lake (Lake Tanganyika).

GREETINGS

• Above all, remember that greetings are *extremely* important. If you fail to greet people and ask about their health and the health of their family, you will be regarded as so rude as to be beneath consideration. This custom applies not only to people you meet socially or at work but also to people in shops, offices, and banks. Even if you're rushing for a bus, saying, "Is this the bus to X" may produce no response. If, despite your rush, you stop and exchange greetings politely, the difference in treatment will be startling. Westerners may find this practice inconvenient, but if you want a positive response from Tanzanians, adhere to it.

• If possible, exchange greetings in Swahili. (See "Key Phrases.") If you don't know Swahili, exchange lengthy greetings in English and/or say "Hello" (sah-**lahm**-ah) and "How are you?" (hah-**bah**-ree) in Swahili.

• To show respect, use the titles "Doctor," "Professor," and "Teacher," when appropriate. Address people who don't have a professional title as "Mr.," "Mrs.," or "Miss" with the last name.

• Close friends show respect by using a person's last name with no title.

• Don't expect people to smile when you meet. This is not a signal of unfriendliness; Tanzanians regard it as polite behavior. In fact, people who smile a great deal at a first meeting are a bit suspect.

• Address old men as *mzee* and older women as *mama.*

• Be aware that people shake hands in greeting, both with members of the same sex and the opposite sex.

• Note that close friends—men and men, men and women, and women and women—hug in greeting.

• Take an interest in the Tanzanians as people. Don't keep talking about the national parks with wild animals, which are the country's major tourist attraction.

• Men should refrain from discussing a woman's pregnancy with her, because this will be seen as rude. Close women friends, however, may bring up the subject.

• Don't comment on the poverty you observe. Tanzania has been financially ruined by the war fought to rid the country of Uganda's Idi Amin.

• In addition, don't comment on the high prices. Much has to be imported, and it's very bad taste to comment, since your income is probably at least 20 times greater than Tanzanians'.

CONVERSATION

• The official languages are Swahili and English. Swahili, derived from Bantu, shows influences of Arabic, Hindi, English, and Portuguese. Most people connected with tourism or international business speak English.

• Don't ask someone what his work is.

• Don't discuss money or salaries. North Americans are invariably thought to be rich.

TELEPHONES

• Most pay phones don't work. It's best to go to the post office to make phone calls or to send telexes and faxes. To make an international call, give the operator the number, go into a booth when you are summoned, and pay when you have finished the call.

• For emergency—police, fire, ambulance—call 999.

IN PUBLIC

• Avoid using the left hand when giving or receiving a business card, a gift, an envelope, etc.

• Don't point with a finger or your hand. With your mouth closed, point your chin in the direction you wish to indicate.

• Expect Tanzanians to be dignified and quiet.

• Note that the more highly educated a person is, the more he or she tends to be punctual.

• Don't take photographs in Dar es Salaam. Many buildings are off-limits, and you have no way of knowing which ones they are. If you were to photograph one of these buildings inadvertently, police could confiscate your camera.

In fact, it's best not to carry a camera in the city, since the police might seize it.

• Ask permission before photographing anyone.

• Around the game parks, many Masai and others pose for pictures. Don't show such photos to Tanzanians, who might feel that you are treating Africans on the same level as animals.

• Bargain everywhere except in restaurants and government gift shops, where the prices are fixed.

• If you would like to trade in markets where crafts are sold, bring with you inexpensive watches, small jackknives, hats, etc.

DRESS

• Tanzanians tend to dress simply, but they are always very clean. Walking around in dirty jeans or grimy clothes will gain you no respect. If you appear unkempt in a bank or business office, you will probably be treated with contempt.

• Women should be very conservative in dress because of the large Muslim population. Be sure that shoulders are covered. Don't wear see-through blouses or miniskirts. Skirts are preferable to shorts, except on beaches or in game reserves.

• For casual attire, pants and a blouse are acceptable for women; men should wear pants and a shirt.

• Even on formal occasions (e.g., a dinner with the President), dress is eclectic. Some men may appear in tuxedos and women in long gowns; some men may wear suits and women short dresses; other men may come simply in shirts and pants.

• Women wearing bathing suits on beaches will probably be hassled if they are alone.

MEALS

Hours and Foods

Breakfast: Between 6:00 and 8:00 A.M. The usual meal is bread with either tea or coffee. In the countryside, people often eat cornmeal gruel.

Lunch: In the countryside, people eat a lunch of *ugali* (cornmeal mush) and cooked greens at about noon. In the cities, between 1:00 and 2:00 P.M., lunch is usually chicken with french fries or rice.

Dinner: About 7:00 or 8:00 P.M., people will dine on rice with beans or on curries.

• Expect beef, goat, and chicken to be served charcoal-broiled or in stews or curries.

• A meal for guests usually features chicken with *ugali* or rice.

• Don't be surprised to be offered hot tea (which will be very sweet) *before* a meal or after the meal.

• If you're invited to dinner in a city, you will be offered beer or soda before the meal but not food, except possibly for peanuts.

• The local alcoholic beverage, *Konyagi,* is a cross between gin and vodka.

• Beer is often served warm or slightly cool, while sodas are usually served cold.

• Don't drink local water or have ice in your drink. Never eat fruits or vegetables that cannot be peeled.

on the floor or on stools around the table, where they will eat with the right hand from a communal bowl. People of the upper classes typically eat with a spoon and fork.

• Tanzanians believe that you haven't visited unless you've eaten. If you aren't hungry or don't care for a certain food, just take tiny bites from the communal bowl.

• To be polite, ask permission before smoking.

• Plan to stay at least 30 minutes after dinner. If the conversation is lively, feel free to stay an hour or a bit more.

Table Manners

• Note that in villages women and children normally eat near the cookfire, especially if there are guests.

• Wait for your host or hostess to seat you, because a certain place may be reserved for the head of the family.

• Expect a pitcher of water to be brought to the eating area for washing hands before the meal. If there are several courses, the ritual will be repeated.

• Realize that food may be served on a tray, which is put on a table or a chair. People may sit

Eating Out

• You'll find a variety of cuisines available in Dar es Salaam: Continental, Arabic, Indian, Chinese, or African. (Whatever type of restaurant you choose, you will probably find an emphasis on fish.)

• Note that African food is not usually spicy, but Indian and Arabic dishes are.

• Menus are not usually posted outside restaurants, except at hotel restaurants, which are the most expensive.

• Realize that menus are more often theoretical than realistic— that is, actually only one or two dishes on the menu may be available. Before making a choice, ask what the day's selections are. Most often, you may choose either *wali kuku* (chicken and rice) or *wali nyama* (beef and rice). Sometimes, instead of rice, *ugali* (cornmeal mush) or *ndizi* (mashed green bananas) will be offered.

• To summon the waiter, say "*Rafiki*" (rah-**fee**-kee), which is the Swahili word for "friend," or with the palm of your hand up, say "Psst."

Specialties

• The following are dishes special in Tanzania: *ndizi na nyama*—a stew of plantains, onions, tomatoes, and coconut milk, with beef if the family can afford it; *wali na samaki*—a peppery mixture made with fried fish and served on rice with vegetables; *sambusa*—an Arabic dish made of spicy ground beef and served in a pastry shell; *mandadi*—like fried dough.

HOTELS

• Realize that there are very few good hotels, except for those in Arusha. However, game lodges usually offer excellent facilities.

• Remember that the Swahili words for "guest house" are *nyumba ya wageni.* If you ask for a *hoteli,* you'll be directed to a restaurant.

• Prepare to pay for the best hotels in hard currency. These hotels have private bathrooms with hot water and air-conditioning; some have swimming pools and very good restaurants. Breakfast is included in the room rate. You will probably be offered a 50% discount between the day after Easter and June 30.

• Avoid the middle-range hotels. Most are unsafe, in poor condition, and have only cold water in the rooms. Most of these hotels, which can be paid in local currency, include a breakfast of bread and coffee.

• In Dar es Salaam, there is a YWCA with very basic facilities (no hot water), which is safe. Men who are with spouses may stay there.

• For budget accommodations, seek out guest houses, which are usually the choice of local people. Most often, they have small rooms, a reception area, and a restaurant. Toilets are of the squat type. The bathroom may be a room with a bucket of cold water, but it may have a shower. Some proprietors will give you a basin of hot water if you ask for it. The majority of guest houses are clean and pleasant, with those run by women tending to be cleaner and more hospitable.

• In Dar es Salaam, don't be surprised at electricity cuts lasting for as long as a few hours. In addition, water runs for only half the day. When you get to your room, if the water is running, take advantage of it, and bathe immediately.

• Staying at an older hotel, you may find that there is no plug for the bathtub. Since most moderately priced and cheap hotels don't have hot water, you may not want to fill the tub anyway.

TIPPING

• Most restaurants and hotels add a service charge. If service is outstanding, you might add the equivalent of 10 to 30 cents U.S.

• Give a porter the equivalent of 25 cents U.S. per bag.

• Don't tip taxi drivers.

• Tip household help the equivalent of $5.00 U.S. for a one-week stay.

• Give a safari guide and the driver the equivalent of $3.00 U.S. per day.

ers, chocolate, liquor, and tapes (if you're bringing video tapes, bring blank ones, unless you know that the family has a system that will play tapes made in North America).

PRIVATE HOMES

• Recognize working schedules by visiting around 5:00 P.M. or on weekends. Since most people don't have phones, just drop in for a visit.

• If you want to enter a home in a village, stand outside and shout, *"Hodi"* (**ho**-dee)—literally, "May I come in?" The response will be *"Hodi"* or *"Karibu"* (kah-**ree**-boo)—meaning "Welcome."

• Since most middle- and upper-class homes have help, don't offer to assist with chores. If you're staying with a village family, offer to help.

• In cities, most bathrooms don't have tubs but do have showers.

Gifts: To a family in the countryside, bring sugar or salt.

• From abroad, bring clothing or practical gifts such as Swiss army knives or watches. Other good gifts from abroad are sneak-

BUSINESS

Hours

Businesses: Monday through Friday, 8:00 A.M. to 12:30 P.M. and 2:00 to 4:00 P.M., and Saturday, 8:00 A.M. to 12:30 P.M.

Banks: Monday through Friday, 8:30 A.M. to 12:30 P.M., and Saturday, 8:30 to 11:30 A.M.

Government Offices: Monday through Friday, 8:00 A.M. to 3:00 P.M. Government employees take a lunch break between 1:00 and 2:00 P.M. The offices are open, but no one will be available to meet with you.

Stores: Monday through Friday, 8:00 A.M. to 12:30 P.M. and 2:00 to 4:00 P.M., and Saturday, 8:00 A.M. to 12:30 P.M.

Money

• The unit of currency is the Tanzanian shilling, abbreviated TSh. A shilling is made up of 100 senti.

• Coins: 5, 10, 20, and 50 senti; 1, 5, 10, and 20 shillings.

• Notes (Bills): 5, 10, 20, 50, 100, and 200 shillings.

• On arrival you'll be issued a currency declaration form; officials may ask to see your cash and traveler's checks. Whenever you change money, *be sure* to have the amount stamped on the form, since you will need to present the form at Customs when you leave Tanzania.

• If you find yourself short of money when banks are closed, remember that hotels will cash traveler's checks. Again, be sure to have your currency form stamped and to retain the receipts.

• Don't change money on the black market. You may be cheated either by being given less money than you were supposed to get or by being given counterfeit money.

• Expect credit cards—Diners Club, American Express, and less frequently, VISA—to be accepted only at major hotels. You must pay in hard currency for airline tickets, for many hotel accommodations, and for all national park camping and entry fees.

• Bring small denominations of hard currency, since you'll be given change in Tanzanian shillings.

Business Practices

• To make contacts, get in touch with the Dar es Salaam Chamber of Commerce, the Rotary Club in Dar es Salaam, U.S. Aid for International Development (USAID), or the U.S. Information Service (USIS) at the U.S. Embassy. In London, contact the Commercial Section of the Tanzanian Embassy. In Ottawa, contact the Commercial Section of the Tanzanian Embassy.

• Make appointments, in the morning if possible, a month in advance. Avoid the weeks before and after Christmas.

• Bring business cards with you (in English). The printing quality in Tanzania isn't good, and the paper stock is of poor quality.

• Realize that it takes about a week to get copies made, so you may wish to bring photocopies with you.

• Be prepared for Tanzanians to be late for meetings.

• Be aware that business is conducted *extremely* slowly, partly becuase of the many layers of bureaucracy.

• Note that business decisions are made by the few people at the top of an organization. Corruption and bribery are often involved in the decisions.

• Expect to have difficulty in obtaining a written contract.

• Don't forget that deadlines are never adhered to.

• Most popular spots for business lunches and dinners are hotel restaurants. Spouses are often included in invitations to business meals.

HOLIDAYS AND SPECIAL OCCASIONS

• The following holidays are observed in Tanzania: Zanzibar Revolution Day (January 12); Founding of the CCM—Freedom Party (February 5); Good Friday; Easter Monday; Union Day (April 26); Labor Day (May 1); Peasants' Day (July 17); Tanzania Independence and Republic Day (December 9); Christmas (December 25).

TRANSPORTATION

Public Transportation

• Taxis are available; however, they are often broken down. They aren't metered, so negotiate the price before getting in. The drivers are very pleasant.

• Book train tickets three days to a week in advance. It's easier to arrange a last-minute ticket on trains going *to* Dar es Salaam than on trains *leaving* it.

• The trains running between Dar es Salaam and Moshi are often unsafe. Robberies have been reported, especially in first-class compartments. To prevent theft through the compartment's window, close all windows at night. If you leave your compartment, take any valuables with you. If you are in a first-class compartment and are reluctant to leave it to go to the dining car, the steward will bring your meals to you.

• In second class, a compartment, which holds six, will be shared by members of the same sex. Men and women may travel together in first or second class on overnight journeys only if they occupy the entire compartment. In third class, there are only seats, with nowhere to sleep. In general, trains are dirty and not well maintained.

• If you take a long-distance bus, don't store your luggage in the overhead compartment or on top of the bus. If you don't put it under your feet or sit on it, the luggage is likely to be stolen.

• Realize that outside of Dar es Salaam, bus schedules are meaningless. Stations are confusing, and no one seems to know when any bus is leaving or arriving. One tourist was told that his bus trip would take from 1½ to 3 hours, It took 5 hours. The bus, built to hold 55, had 120 passengers. It was so crowded that the conductor had to climb over the seats to collect the fares.

• Avoid overnight buses, which have a bad reputation because of theft.

• Never accept food from strangers on buses; it may be drugged.

• Try to avoid the boats called *dhows,* which go to Zanzibar. The trip takes 5 hours and the *dhows* are packed with seasick people.

• If you're traveling a long distance, take a plane. Regularly scheduled daily flights connect major cities and towns. The problem will be getting a ticket. Unless you offer travel agents or airline agents a bribe of TSh 500, they will tell you that the flights are full.

Driving

• Be aware that car rentals are expensive, and rental cars are poorly maintained. Hire a car with a driver instead.

• Drive on the left—as in England.

• Keep in mind that only 10% of the roads are paved, and there are *enormous* potholes, so you'll never drive in a straight line.

• If you hit an animal, keep driving. Even if you would like to pay, it isn't safe to stop.

• Expect major problems in finding parking in the city. There is no infrastructure to support the volume of cars.

• Remember that you aren't allowed to drive in national parks during the hours between 7:00 P.M. and 6:00 A.M.

LEGAL MATTERS, HEALTH, AND SAFETY

• While it is legal in Tanzania to sell ivory, elephant hair bracelets, and other animal products, do not buy them, even if the owner of the shop offers you a certificate attesting that they were legally purchased in Tanzania. Such items cannot be brought into the U.S.

• In remote areas, don't be alarmed if you are stopped by a policeman who wants to check your passport and ask you a few questions. Police are usually friendly. Never act annoyed and imply that you're wasting your time answering their questions.

• Don't walk at night out of town or away from hotels in national park areas because you may encounter dangerous animals.

• Don't carry valuables with you in Dar es Salaam and Bagamoyo, as you could be the victim of a mugger or pickpocket.

• Women should note that it's safer to travel with a fanny pack than with a purse. Be especially careful around beaches.

• If you stay in any of the beach resorts around Dar es Salaam, don't walk along the beach or on roads connecting one beach to another, because people have been robbed there. Take a taxi instead.

• Avoid swimming or wading in rivers, streams, or lakes, because of the risk of the parasitic disease bilharzia.

KEY PHRASES

English	*Swahili Pronounciation*
Hello	sah-**lahm**-ah
Good morning	ha-**bah**-ree yah ah-soo-**boo**-hee
Good day (said around noon)	ha-**bah**-ree mchah-nah
Good evening	ha-**bah**-ree ah-jo-nee
Good-bye	kwah-**hay**-ree
How are you?	hah-**bah**-ree?
Sir	**bwah**-nah
Madame	**bee**-bee
Miss	**bin**-tee
Please	tah-sah-**bah**-lee
Thank you	ah-**sahn**-tay
You're welcome	**see** neh-no
Yes	**ndee**-oh
No	ha-**pah**-na
Excuse me	tah-sah-**bah**-lee
I don't understand	see-eh-**leh**-wee
I don't understand Swahili	see-eh-**leh**-wee kee-swah-**hee**-lee
Do you speak English?	jeh oo-nah-on-**gay**-uh kee in-gay-**ray**-zah?

When you enter a shop, the salesperson may say *"Karibu"* (kah-**ree**-boo), which means "Welcome." The proper response is *"Asante sana"* (ah-**sahn**-tay sah-nah), meaning "Thank you very much."

UGANDA

Although landlocked Uganda boasts such scenic wonders as Lake Victoria, the second largest lake in the world, the country is still trying to live down the negative reputation acquired during the reign of Idi Amin Dada.

To that end, Uganda is trying to get the international community to pay attention to its string of National Game Parks, rich in wildlife and scenery. The crown jewel of this park system is Murchison Falls National Park, through which the River Nile passes and in which many species of birds and other wildlife make their home.

GREETINGS

- Shake hands when greeting and departing. When a new person is introduced to a group, everyone should rise and shake hands.
- Don't be surprised to see women kneel down when greeting men, especially in private homes. They may half kneel when greeting men on the road.
- Use the titles Mr., Mrs., Miss, Doctor, and Professor, when appropriate.
- Expect good friends to hug good friends—of both sexes—in greeting.
- Don't use first names until you know someone well and that person has used your first name.

CONVERSATION

- Note that English is Uganda's official language, but Luganda is the main language, with Swahili also important (although it is not often spoken in Kampala). About 30% of the population understands English.
- Never begin a conversation without greeting the other person and asking how he/she is.
- Remember that speaking softly is a sign of respect.
- Always look at people when you are talking to them. It's considered rude to look away when someone is speaking to you.

• Avoid discussing politics and religion until you are well acquainted with a Ugandan.

• A person's family and job are both good subjects of conversation.

• With women, discuss fashion.

• To talk about sex is taboo either in a mixed group or in public. It is less prohibited among peers.

TELEPHONES

• Realize that the telephone booths on the street are removed at night.

• Use calling cards (AT&T) from public phones, or make calls from the post office.

• From hotels and private homes, direct dialing is possible.

• Keep in mind that you can't make a collect call from Uganda.

• Note that telephone operators speak English.

• For an emergency requiring police, firefighters, or an ambulance, dial 999.

IN PUBLIC

• Note that Ugandans typically are polite and tolerant.

• Always give and accept objects (e.g., a key, food, a book) with the right hand.

• Never display affection in public.

• Office buildings may have "No Smoking" signs posted, but one room is always available for smoking.

• In villages, keep in mind that it is considered vulgar for a woman to smoke.

• Small children in villages may seek your attention by chanting, "Bye-bye." The expression is actually a greeting and doesn't mean that they want you to leave.

• Bargain in markets and small shops but not in first-class stores.

• Always ask permission before photographing people. Most Ugandans enjoy having their picture taken. If you promise someone a copy, be sure to send it, because he/she will truly appreciate it.

• Avoid taking pictures of abject poverty. Ugandans are sensitive on this issue.

• Don't photograph railway stations, airports, military installations, bridges, Parliament, or the Owen Falls Dam in Jinja.

• In cities, you'll find Western-style public bathrooms in restaurants, hotels, and parks.

DRESS

• Note that everyday clothing is usually Western style, but national dress is worn on special occasions (weddings, funerals, and other ceremonies). Ugandans appreciate it when Westerners wear this national dress on such special occasions. For women the national costume is the *busuti*, a long cotton gown with a sash. Men wear the *kanzu*, a long, loose gown with a round neck.

• Remember that Ugandans tend to dress elegantly, so women may feel most comfortable in a dress or skirt, although pants are acceptable for touring. *Always* wear a skirt or dress in villages.

• Men may wear shorts, but women shouldn't.

• At home people of the upper classes often wear jeans or pants, but they dress up when they go out.

• For business, men should wear a suit and tie, and women should wear a suit or dress.

• There are no beaches where it's acceptable to be nude.

MEALS

Hours and Foods

Breakfast: Between 7:00 and 9:00 A.M. The upper classes have a substantial meal of eggs, bacon, bread, and coffee, tea, and passion fruit juice. Lower classes eat *matoke,* which is cooked, mashed green plantain.

Lunch: Between 12:30 and 2:30 P.M. The most popular lunch dish is stewed or roasted beef; other meats served include chicken and pork. Accompanying the meat will be some of the following: rice; peas or beans; *matoke,* cassava, sweet potatoes, or potatoes.

Tea: Sometime between 4:00 and 6:00 P.M. People eat roasted corn on the cob, boiled or roasted cassava, cookies and cakes, and they drink tea.

Some people take tea breaks at 11:00 A.M. and 3:00 P.M., when they snack on roasted peanuts and popcorn.

Dinner: Between 7:00 and 10:00 P.M. This main meal of the day is similar to lunch but features more dishes.

• Note that Ugandans like "sugar bread." Ask for "salt bread" if you would prefer your bread less sweet.

Beverages: With meals Ugandans drink water, juice, and soda. Some families drink beer and wine. Tea is served after meals. Tea and coffee are served with *lots* of milk and sugar. Advise your hosts of your preference. You shouldn't drink the local water or have drinks with ice made from it. Explain to your host that you have a health problem and cannot drink the water.

Table Manners

• Your hosts may offer you a drink before dinner. If you would prefer something nonalcoholic, ask for it. (In some Christian homes there is no alcohol in the house.)

• Wait for your host or hostess to seat you.

• In cities people eat at tables with cutlery, and you'll serve yourself from platters. In villages people sit on a mat on the floor. Banana leaves are put on the mat, and the food is placed on them. The mother then serves each person on individual plates (no eating from a communal bowl here).

• Men usually eat separately from women, often outside.

• Be sure to eat with the right hand. If you don't feel comfortable eating with your hands, you won't offend by asking for a fork or a spoon.

• In upper-class homes, people follow the British pattern of table setting and dining (eating with the knife in the right hand and the fork in the left, etc.).

• Don't smoke without first asking permission.

• Stay about 30 minutes after the meal is finished.

Eating Out

• In Kampala, the capital, you'll find everything from Indian restaurants to Italian pizza eateries. Ask local people where to find one of the clubs serving international foods. You don't have to be a member to eat at one. Universities also have guest houses where you may have meals.

• Expect to find menus posted outside restaurants, European style.

• To attract the waiter's attention, raise your hand.

Specialties

• All over the country people eat *posho* (ground maize flour) and beans; *chapatis* (round, flat Indian bread with wheat flour); *binyebwa* (peanut soup, consisting of ground peanuts with eggplant, mushrooms, onions, tomatoes, and spinach).

• Popular in the north are *lapena* (a dish made with peas) and

malakwang (a groundnut sauce served with greens). Rice is a staple, along with cassava, millet, and potatoes. Sesame paste is used in sauces.

• Popular in the south are *luwombo* (chicken or beef in a sauce, cooked in banana leaves) and *dodo* (a vegetable similar to spinach). The staple is *matoke,* boiled plantain, which is mashed and eaten with an accompaniment of fish, goat, or chicken.

HOTELS

• Note that the Ugandan Hotels Corporation owns a chain of top hotels, but they require payment in hard currency, *not* in Ugandan shillings.

• Top hotels in Kampala have private baths, hot and cold running water, and electricity, with breakfast included in the room price. They also provide secretarial and fax services.

• Most rural hotels do not have running water, and electricity is erratic.

• If you are a student or a scholar working on a project in Uganda, you can arrange in advance to stay at a university guest house.

TIPPING

• At a restaurant, leave 5% to 10% of the check.

• Tip drivers of private taxis 10% of the fare.

• Give porters the equivalent of $1.00 U.S.

• Leave hotel room attendants the equivalent of 25 cents U.S. per day.

PRIVATE HOMES

• Ugandans usually visit after work. If the person you plan to visit has a telephone, call ahead.

• Always enter a home through the *back* door, unless the person you're visiting is very Westernized and educated.

• It's acceptable to sightsee on your own, but if a family suggests taking you around, it would be a good idea to accept their offer at the beginning of your visit so that you can get your bearings.

• Feel free to bathe every day. Upper-class homes will have hot water. In other homes people will give you heated water in a basin. In the bathroom, pour the water over yourself. Your Ugandan hosts will assume you want to bathe at night and will usually give you the heated water at that time. They will probably give you soap and a towel, but you might want to be on the safe side by bringing your own soap.

• A couple of notes on meals with a family: (1) Ask when dinner will be served; families eat together at sometime between 7:00 and 10:00 P.M. (2) Try to eat all the food offered.

Gifts: When invited to a meal in an upper-class home, bring wine or candy. In a village, bring coffee, tea, or cookies.

• If you're staying with a family, give them a practical gift, such as dishes, cups and saucers, blankets, or sheets.

• From abroad bring cameras, digital watches, T-shirts with logos, audio cassettes of pop music for young people, or American cigarettes for men (if you know that they smoke).

BUSINESS

Hours

Businesses: Monday through Friday, 8:00 A.M. to 5:00 P.M., with a lunch break between noon and 2:00 P.M.

Government Offices: Monday through Friday, 8:00 A.M. to 5:00 P.M.

Banks: Monday through Friday, 9:00 A.M. to 2:00 P.M. A few are open on Saturday from 9:00 A.M. to noon.

Stores: Monday through Saturday, 8:00 A.M. to 7:00 P.M. Some small shops may stay open until midnight.

Money

• The unit of currency is the Ugandan shilling (abbreviated USh), made up of 100 cents.

• Coins: 10, 25 cents (coins aren't really used because of inflation).

• Notes (Bills): 10, 20, 100, and 500 shillings.

• Use credit cards with airlines, hotels, shops for foreigners, and at first-class restaurants.

• When you enter Uganda, you'll be issued a Currency Declaration Form. Be sure to have it stamped every time you change money, even though the forms aren't always checked when you leave the country. You may be asked to produce the form at roadblocks within Uganda.

• You won't be allowed in any national park unless your Currency Declaration Form has at least one stamp—showing that you have changed money at least once.

Business Practices

• Seek initial contacts through the Lions Club or the Rotary Club if you are a member, or the Kampala Chamber of Commerce in Uganda.

• From abroad make appointments two weeks in advance.

• Avoid suggesting meetings during the week between Christmas and New Year's Day. Offices are open, but most people aren't there, and nothing gets accomplished.

• Since English is the national language, an interpreter won't be necessary.

• Facilities for photocopying are available.

• To enhance your presentation, bring graphics and visuals.

• Don't expect an initial period of social chat (i.e., people wanting to get to know you) before business.

• Be aware that bribery is common everywhere in order to accomplish an objective.

• Even though there are women lawyers and women heads of government and banking departments, companies generally prefer to do business with men.

• Don't include spouses in business invitations unless they are part of the business.

• Business lunches are more common than dinners, with hotel restaurants being the most popular places for business entertaining.

HOLIDAYS AND SPECIAL OCCASIONS

• Uganda celebrates the following holidays: New Year's Day (January 1); Liberation Day (April 11); Good Friday; Easter Monday; Labor Day (May 1); Independence Day (October 9); Christmas (December 25 and 26).

• A holiday that varies with the Muslim calendar is *Id al-Fitr* (the end of Ramadan).

TRANSPORTATION

Public Transportation

• *Matatus,* shared taxis that travel within and between cities, are found in special car parks. Fares are based on distance.

• The private taxis, called "specials," are also located in selected car parks. Since they don't have meters, negotiate the fare in advance.

• Buses are crowded, but they're safer than *matatus.* They run less frequently than *matatus,* though. Pay when you get on, and keep your ticket, since inspectors may check.

• Train service within the country is very poor. There are many breakdowns and derailments. In bathrooms trash is strewn everywhere. In first class, you'll find a small compartment with two berths. Second class is the same as first but with six berths. Economy class offers very crowded seating. In first and second class, the sexes are separated, unless your group fills a compartment. Book a day in advance for first and second class. First make a reservation and then get in line to pay.

• Most trains have dining cars where meals, soft drinks, and beer are available. The dining cars are more comfortable than the crowded compartments. Since there are often no connecting doors between compartments and the dining car, you must wait until the train stops to come and go.

• At most train stations there are food stands that sell roasted maize, barbecued meat, *ugali* (maize meal), fruit, coffee, and tea.

• For transportation within Uganda, your best bet probably is to fly.

Driving

• Although you can rent cars at hotels, it's much cheaper (and better) to rent a car *and* driver. If you are driving yourself, you're responsible for damages. Other problems with driving yourself: (1) Ugandans tend to drive recklessly, and you have to drive very aggressively in order to survive. (2) Street signs may not be clear, so you'll have to ask for directions. (3) Maps may be old, and the names of streets, roads, and towns, etc., may have changed.

• Remember that driving is on the left, as in Great Britain.

• Be aware that minor roads are filled with potholes and are impassable after heavy rains.

• Seat belts are not compulsory.

• In most places, parking is free.

will probably not be available in other areas.

• Don't swim in lakes or rivers, because of the risk of bilharzia. Don't go barefoot in areas where there are reeds. The snails that are the intermediate host for the parasite that causes bilharzia live in these areas.

• Be careful if someone approaches you and starts chatting— he/she may be a pickpocket. The risk is especially great in Kampala.

LEGAL MATTERS, HEALTH, AND SAFETY

• Keep in mind that police tend to be lenient with foreigners.

• Uganda has no black market.

• Don't drink the local water or have ice in drinks. Don't eat fruits or vegetables that can't be peeled.

• Take bottled water with you if you're leaving Kampala, since it

ZIMBABWE

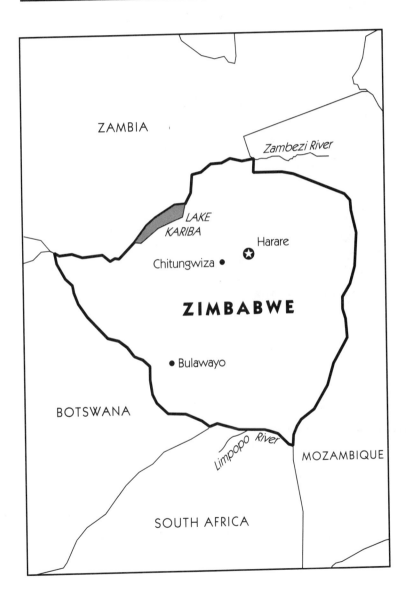

If one had to summarize Zimbabwe in one word, it would have to be "spectacular." No one who has gazed on the great cascade of Victoria Falls will ever forget that catch of breath as the Falls first came into view.

Visitors to the Great Zimbabwe Ruins will marvel over the people who built this enormous stone city, which housed 10,000 people hundreds of years ago. Like the creators of the great Mayan cities in Mexico and Stonehenge in England, their identities are lost in the mists of time.

Another splendor is the carving of the Shona sculptors, whose art has drawn critics' praise throughout the world. As *Newsday* columnist Les Payne explained, "The art, which takes its name from the people who make up 80 percent of the population of Zimbabwe, is a free-form carving from serpentine stone (found only in Zimbabwe). The creators take their inspiration from mountain springs, animals running free, humans at work, the wind rustling through leaves."

GREETINGS

• Remember that shaking hands when first meeting someone is very important. Greetings will take a long time; you must inquire how a person is and ask about every family member.

• Good friends of both sexes and men and women who are friends shake hands in greeting. Only *extremely* good friends ever hug.

• Don't be surprised if a woman or girl curtsies in greeting.

• Never look older people in the eye when greeting them.

• Most often, people greet each other with a handshake and a clapping of hands. In a more traditional setting, women get on their knees and men crouch on their toes as they clap and ask about one another's families' health.

• As a sign of respect, women genuflect when they shake hands or give something to another person.

• Don't use first names until a Zimbabwean has used yours.

CONVERSATION

• Note that English is the official language, but the major languages are Shona, spoken by 60% to 70% of the people, and Ndebele, spoken by 15% to 20% of the people. Shona is spoken in the Harare area, and Ndebele in the Bulawayo area.

• Because of the many years of colonialism, black Zimbabweans may address white women as "Madame" and white men as "Boss." If you don't feel comfortable being addressed this way, ask people to call you by your first name.

• Avoid discussing political and economic conditions.

• If you are Caucasian, realize that black people will be suspicious if you ask them their political views. However, blacks from North America may discuss politics.

• In your first conversation, don't ask about a person's job or whether he/she is married.

• Ask advice on what to see or do. Zimbabweans will be interested in offering suggestions.

• Another good subject is families. Zimbabweans will be curious about yours and will be pleased by your interest in theirs.

• Because people tend to tell you what you want to hear, be sure to phrase questions so you'll elicit the desired response. For example, instead of asking how far something is, ask, "How long does it take to go to X place walking or by bike?" (People tend to think in terms of time rather than distance.)

• Two terms that may appear in conversation: "High-density suburbs" refers to former townships, and "low-density suburbs" to nicer areas.

• Blacks will not be offended if you bring up the subject of race relations.

• If you're an African-American, realize that Zimbabweans in rural areas may have difficulty understanding why you can't speak the local languages. They erroneously may conclude that you are conceited.

TELEPHONES

• You'll find public phone booths on the street, but many don't work, and you may wait hours in line to find that the lines are busy. The wait will be especially long in Harare and Bulawayo.

• Local calls cost Z15c for three minutes.

• If you want to talk for a long time on a public phone, line up several coins in the slots, and they will drop in automatically.

• Don't look for separate telephone offices to make international calls. They don't exist in Zimbabwe.

• Some options for making international calls: (1) Book the call through the front desk of a hotel; however, you will be charged two to three times what the call costs. (2) Go to the post office, although it may be crowded and the wait may be long. (3) Make the call from a public phone. You'll need

stacks of Z$1 coins. (4) Call collect from a private home. (That's the only place you can make collect calls—and then only to a few countries.) Whether you call collect or wish to pay for the call, you may have a hard time getting through to an operator, who will call you back when the call goes through. The wait may be a long one.

• Don't be surprised if you have a better connection on an overseas call than on a local call. During the rainy season the internal lines worsen.

• For police, fire, or ambulance in an emergency, dial 99. For non-emergency police matters, call 733033.

IN PUBLIC

• Realize that Zimbabweans tend to be late, but they expect Westerners to be on time.

• Be sure to treat older people with great respect. Be very courteous, and never question their word. Treat teachers, doctors, and other professionals with similar deference.

• Avoid backslapping.

• Clapping hands is a signal of thanks.

• Refrain from displays of intimacy in public, and don't be overly familiar with a man's female relatives.

• Ask permission before smoking.

• If you're traveling with children, realize that it's rude for them to occupy a seat on a bus if adults are standing.

• A woman traveling alone may be regarded with suspicion, because people will wonder why she's not at home with her husband and children.

• Always ask permission before taking a photograph of a person or a small group. People may ask to be paid. Some may refuse, and others may ask you to take their photos—children love to have their pictures taken.

• Be aware that many restaurants in cities have flush toilets, but in what used to be the townships there are squat-type toilets with no toilet paper.

• Don't bargain in the Western-style stores, where prices are fixed. Feel free to bargain in markets, but don't start negotiating for

something you don't intend to buy.

DRESS

• Note that in the city people dress up. In rural areas, don't dress up because you'll be immediately be pegged as "the rich foreigner."

• Zimbabwe does not have a traditional costume; dress is completely Westernized.

• It's acceptable for women to wear pants, but skirts will make a better impression, especially in rural areas. However, the pants should be loose-fitting—never tight stretch pants. Women should also be careful that none of their clothing is revealing.

• For business in cities, men should wear suits and ties, and women should wear dresses or suits.

• Realize that many restaurants and bars have a dress code. Men must wear shirts, not T-shirts, and neither sex may wear tennis shoes or sandals. Call ahead to learn if the restaurant you intend to patronize has such a code.

• Be aware that camouflage dress is illegal.

MEALS

Hours and Foods

Breakfast: In cities, about 7:00 A.M. In villages, the meal, eaten sometime between 7:00 and 8:00 A.M., consists of *bota* (a porridge), bread or fried dough, and tea with milk and sugar.

Lunch: Between noon and 1:00 P.M. in cities and around 1:00 P.M. in villages. The content of the meal is determined by the class of the diners. At lunch or dinner, upper-class people have rice pilaf, steak or grilled chicken, and salad (other groups don't eat salad). Members of the middle class will have rice, potatoes, or *sadza* (cornmeal porridge), with beef or chicken and cabbage, rape (similar to kale), or pumpkin leaves. Villagers or those of the lower class eat *sadza* with collard greens, okra, or sour milk. If they have enough money, there will be a little meat in the vegetables. *Nyama* is a generic term for meat; it refers to beef, goat, mutton, and chicken.

To eat *sadza,* dip it into the milk or greens.

Dinner: In both cities and villages people eat about 7:00 P.M. The foods are interchangeable with those at lunch.

• Chicken is a staple of the Zimbabwean diet, and beef is widely available. In rural areas, people often eat mutton and goat.

• Among the upper and middle classes, the most popular drinks are wine and beer. Beer isn't drunk with meals but either after the meal or at other times of the day when people are socializing. Wine is a luxury reserved for special dinners. With meals, water and sometimes Coca-Cola are served. (It's safe to drink the water.) After the meal in a village, you'll be offered a home brew made from sorghum.

• Realize that the best tea and coffee grown in the country are exported. In most hotels, "Day-break"—a mixture of instant coffee and chicory—is served. (Most travelers find it revolting.) A very good tea is available everywhere: Nyanga.

• Popular nonalcoholic drinks: Malawi shandy—ginger beer, Angostura, soda water, lemon, and ice; Rock shandy—the same, except that lemonade is substituted for ginger beer; *maheu*—a traditional, sweet, nonalcoholic drink made from corn or sorghum malt.

• In cities, tea with bread and jam is served around 3:00 or 4:00 P.M. In offices tea is delivered to the workers.

• Alcoholic drinks: (1) The alcoholic drink of "the masses" is *chibuku,* which is served in buckets. It's made from yeast, millet, sorghum and *mealie* meal. You can't order it in a pub. It's drunk principally in the high-density-suburb beer halls. (2) "Doro," the traditional beer, is brewed commercially.

• Note that most beer is not labeled. You have to look at the bottle cap for the brand name.

Table Manners

• Expect Zimbabweans who live in cities to replicate British man-ners—e.g., the table setting will be British style, and people will keep the knife in the right hand and the fork in the left.

• Realize that in villages men and boys eat together, and women and daughters eat together. As a guest, you'll be given a separate plate and won't be expected to eat from the communal bowl. (In cities families eat together at a table.)

• Before the meal, prepare to wash your hands in the water you'll be given. Sometimes your hostess will pour the water over your hands. If you don't see the water, ask for it.

• Remember that in traditional homes silverware is not used.

• Eat only with your right hand.

• Note that gobbling your food or failing to share it with others is considered rude.

Eating Out

• In Harare and Bulawayo, you'll find restaurants of many nationalities near the business district—Indian, Chinese, Greek, Italian, etc.

• Most eating places follow the practice of posting menus outside.

• Seek out the larger hotels for huge luncheon buffets.

• If you buy a bottled beverage,

prepare to pay a high deposit. Cheaper places will generally allow you to buy a bottle only if you bring an empty to exchange. There are strict laws concerning bottle conservation, and places must supply as many empties to the distributor as they purchase.

Specialties

• Some popular dishes in Zimbabwe: *biltong,* a snack of dried meat—beef, kudu, or ostrich—which is very salty; game meat, such as crocodile, impala, or kudu, when they are available; trout, in the eastern highlands; bream, the most popular fish; *kapenta,* a dried, anchovy-like fish.

HOTELS

• Keep in mind that middle- to upper-range hotels are rated from one to five stars. Most of the mid-range hotels have one or two stars. In four- and five-star hotels, foreigners must pay in U.S. dollars and will be charged a higher rate than residents of Zimbabwe. At less-expensive hotels, Zimbabwe dollars will be accepted, providing you have bank exchange slips (which you get when you exchange money) for the amount of the bill.

• Book from your country to save the 10% hotel tax.

• Avoid the cheapest hotels. They're used for sex and drinking—and are noisy. However, there's really no need to seek a cheap hotel, since even the luxurious ones are reasonably priced.

• Note that there are youth hostels in Harare and Bulawayo.

• Don't be surprised if Zimbabweans offer to let you stay with them.

• The bed-and-breakfast idea is just beginning to catch on. Most B&Bs are modeled on the British style—a room in someone's private home.

• National Park lodges, cottages, and chalets—usually set in beautiful areas of the parks—are reasonably priced and offer self-catering accommodations in one- or two-bedroom units. They are furnished, have sheets and towels, and have cooking equipment.

• An excellent value for meals are the buffets offered at breakfast and lunch by hotels.

• Prepare to pay very high prices for European food, which is offered by all the large tourist hotels.

TIPPING

• At restaurants, leave 10% of the bill.

• Give taxi drivers 10% of the fare.

• Tip porters the equivalent of 25 cents U.S.

• Give hotel room attendants and household help in private homes the equivalent of $1.25 U.S. per week.

PRIVATE HOMES

• Feel free to drop in for a visit. Phone service is unreliable, so it's difficult to call ahead. About 50% of people in urban areas have telephones.

• Don't be surprised if people, even those of modest means, have servants and gardeners.

• Realize that average people in cities live in very crowded conditions. If you're staying with a city family, prepare to share a bedroom.

• Be aware that there is constant hot water in homes of the wealthy and middle class. Poor people have to heat their water.

• If you're staying with a family in a village, offer to help with cooking and cleaning. They probably won't allow you to, but your gesture shows that you want to be part of the family.

Gifts: Villagers appreciate clothing—even used clothing.

The size doesn't matter, because someone in the family will be able to wear it.

• If you give money to people in villages, always say something such as, "Buy some sugar for your children's porridge" or "Buy some school supplies for your children." Give the equivalent of $2.00 U.S. for a few days' stay with a family.

• From abroad, bring tapes of British black musicians. Zimbabweans listen to the BBC and know all the current pop singers; they aren't so familiar with American black artists. Another item to consider bringing from abroad is digital watches, which are very expensive in Zimbabwe.

• Give children toys, dolls, books, T-shirts.

• Be sure to give and accept gifts with both hands.

BUSINESS

Hours

Businesses: Monday through Friday, 8:00 A.M. to 5:00 P.M., and 8:00 A.M. to noon on Saturday.

Government Offices: Monday through Friday, 8:00 A.M. to 5:00 P.M.; closed Saturday.

Banks: Monday through Friday, 8:30 A.M. to 2:00 P.M., except for Wednesday, when they close at noon, and Saturday, 8:30 to 11:00 A.M.

Stores: Monday through Friday, 8:00 A.M. to 5:00 P.M. (some places close early on Wednesday), with a lunch break between 1:00 and 2:00 P.M., and Saturday, 8:00 A.M. to noon.

Money

• The unit of currency is the Zimbabwe dollar (Z$), made up of 100 cents.

• Coins: 1, 5, 10, 20, 50 cents, and Z$1.

• Notes (Bills): Z$2, Z$5, Z$10, and Z$20.

• When you enter the country, you'll be given a book that *must* be stamped every time you exchange money in a bank. Be prepared to show the book at Customs when you leave.

• Don't change more money than you think you will spend, since Zimbabwean currency is not convertible.

• Note that there is no restriction on the amount of foreign currency that may be brought in and declared, but only Z$40 may be brought into the country or taken out.

• Avoid the black market. Penalties are severe if you are caught using it.

• Use your credit cards with airlines, hotels, *some* better restaurants, and large stores. In general, however, cash is needed in shops and at all but the best restaurants.

Business Practices

• For contacts in Zimbabwe, get in touch with the Chief Public Relations Officer at the Zimbabwe Chamber of Commerce, or the Ministry of Industry and Commerce, or the Confederation of Zimbabwe Industries. All are based in Harare, the capital.

• Avoid business trips in June. It's the quietest, coolest month, and many businesses close, since there is so little activity. Also avoid Independence Day (April 18) and Heroes' Day (August 11 and 12), because people usually take long weekends.

• Don't hire a translator. English is widely spoken.

• Be sure to bring an adequate supply of business cards, since it's difficult to get them printed in Zimbabwe.

• If you need to send a telex, go to the post office. Most big businesses in Zimbabwe have telex machines.

• To send a fax, go to a bank or travel agency. There are few fax machines in Zimbabwe.

• Look for photocopy machines in little shops, such as bookstores, places where magazines are sold, and libraries.

• Be punctual. Professional people tend to be on time, but others may not be.

• Always accept the tea that you will be offered at the beginning of a business meeting.

• Remember that personal relationships are extraordinarily important; don't become impatient with a long period of personal conversation.

• Realize that business is conducted very slowly, partly because of paperwork and bureaucracy, and partly because people must check with their superiors before making a commitment. If something cannot be done, you probably won't be given an explanation as to why.

• Expect to find few women in the upper echelons of the business world, outside of the cosmetics industry and beauty salons.

• To entertain a Zimbabwean colleague, choose a hotel restaurant.

HOLIDAYS AND SPECIAL OCCASIONS

• The following public holidays are observed in Zimbabwe: New Year's Day (January 1); Good Friday, Easter Sunday, Easter Monday; Independence Day (April 18); Workers' Day (May 1); Africa Days (May 25 and 26); Heroes' Day and Defense Forces Day (August 11 and 12); Christmas (December 25); Boxing Day (December 26).

• For Christmas, the biggest holiday of the year, Zimbabweans buy new outfits. People in villages slaughter a goat or a cow. They eat it with a great deal of bread. (The only other time that people eat so much meat is at a wedding.)

TRANSPORTATION

Public Transportation

• Realize that public transportation in cities is a problem. At 5:00 P.M., all offices close, and everyone leaves at once. Since there aren't enough buses or taxis, people have to wait for a very long time.

• Try to take taxis in cities. They are readily available and are relatively inexpensive.

• You may want to avoid the shared taxis (called "emergency vehicles"), which run along specific routes. They are usually old station wagons into which as many people as possible are crammed. There is a set fare.

• Intra-city buses are extremely crowded and don't run as often as emergency vehicles.

• To travel a long distance by bus, take a coach, which will be air-conditioned. Reserve in advance. You can take a chance on buying a ticket at the last minute, but you may find the bus sold out. Note that the regular long-distance buses are very slow, and animals are often passengers.

• Although there aren't many train lines, some luxurious accommodations are available. The Rhodesian Railways sleeping cabin train has dark wood, green leather seats, and etched glass. with sinks in each cabin, a bathroom at the end of each car, and a dining car. Two to four passengers share sleeping cabins with bunk beds. If you'll be traveling at a popular time, purchase tickets well in advance.

• The sexes are separated at night in trains with sleeping compartments, unless you reserve a family compartment or a coupe (two-person compartment) in advance and pay an additional charge. Although second-class compartments are supposed to be for six adult passengers, children aren't counted, so the compartments can be quite cramped.

• Consider taking one of the inexpensive flights within the country. Tourists can get package deals with four or five stops.

Driving

• If you're staying 90 days or less, a driver's license from your country is sufficient.

• Book well in advance if you wish to rent a car, since rentals are in short supply.

• Be aware that you must be at least 23 years old to rent a car.

• Drive on the left, as in England.

• Note that the usual speed limit is 60 kph (about 35 mph) in urban areas and 100 kph (60 mph) on open roads. However, watch for signs that may show a different speed limit.

• Realize that street names are constantly changing, causing great confusion for drivers. You will probably have to stop often to ask for directions.

• In Harare expect metered parking all around the city and parking garages in some areas.

• Be very watchful for game (e.g., antelope and elephant) wandering into the road. In rural areas, people often have their animals on the road. If you kill an animal, you must compensate the owner.

LEGAL MATTERS, HEALTH, AND SAFETY

• Don't be surprised to be asked for food or money by the police at roadblocks. You may or may not give something to them, but you won't be hassled if you don't. In general, the Zimbabwean police aren't as intimidating as the police in other African countries.

• Women should realize that they are liable to be arrested if they swim topless.

• Feel free to drink the tap water in Zimbabwe. If you buy fruits or vegetables, be sure to wash them *well* before eating.

• Be cautious, especially at night, in bus terminals, discos, and large parks in Harare and Bulawayo. Pickpockets are a major problem. Wear a money belt or use a little bag that can be worn under a shirt.

• Don't walk alone at night between Bulawayo's city center and the camping grounds.

• Note that campgrounds and caravan parks have guards to watch over campers' belongings. Even so, don't leave anything valuable in your tent.

• Stay away from the Mozambique border.

• If you're traveling in the eastern highlands, be conscious of the danger of land mines left by rebels from Mozambique and by the Zimbabwe military. If you are off the beaten path in this area, don't touch anything that looks like a weapon.

• In general, women are safe traveling alone. They have the freedom of Zimbabwean men in rural areas. For example, local women would not go to bars, but it's acceptable for foreign women to do so. However, a woman—whether black or white—should not go alone into working-class beer halls or beer gardens.

• Women should bring with them whatever personal hygiene products they use. Tampons are rarely available, and local brands are inferior.

• Women should not use public transportation and should guard against the frequent purse-snatching in downtown Harare.

• In Bulawayo, the second largest city, women should avoid the remote sections of Centenary and Central parks, even in the daytime.

ABOUT THE AUTHORS

We have written five other travel books: *The Travelers' Guide to European Customs and Manners, The Travelers' Guide to Asian Customs and Manners, The Travelers' Guide to Latin American Customs and Manners, The Travelers' Guide to Middle Eastern and North African Customs and Manners,* and *European Customs and Manners.*

Writing this book has involved countless hours of interviews, as well as visits to exotic ports of call neither of us ever expected to see.

Elizabeth Devine lives in Marblehead, Massachusetts. She is a professor of English at Salem State College, where she teaches courses in Feature Writing, Travel Writing, and Mystery Fiction. She has edited reference books, and in addition to the travel books on which she has collaborated with Ms. Braganti, she has written travel and feature articles for such publications as *TV Guide, Boston Magazine, The New York Times,* the *Boston Globe,* and the *Chicago Tribune.*

Nancy L. Braganti has taught foreign languages in the U.S., Europe, and the Middle East. She has traveled extensively in Africa. Ms. Braganti is currently working at the Marblehead Library and is involved with an ongoing campaign for material aid and school supplies for South Africa and Central America in conjunction with the American Friends Service Committee. She lives in Marblehead, Massachusetts, with her husband, Fausto. Her daughter, Tanya, a photographer, is "on the road."